Upper Peninsula

Amazing and Historic Locations
From the Bridge to the Keweenaw

◦ETAOIN PUBLISHING◦
www.etaoinpublishing.com

HURON
PHOTO.COM

Publisher: Etaoin Publishing and Huron Photo LLC
             Saginaw, MI
             www.EtaoinPublishing.com
             www.HuronPhoto.com

ISBN 978-1-955474-13-9

Thank You to all the Yoopers I have met
while Lost In The Upper Peninsula

Introduction

I have been traveling around the Upper Peninsula for many decades and over the past several years for my website Lost In Michigan. I have visited many popular tourist destinations as well as out of the way places that few people know about. I like to visit unconventional locations such as old cemeteries, the crumbling remains of an old mine or the forgotten buildings of an old ghost town. The Upper Peninsula is an outdoor paradise and referred to by some as "God's Country" for the many idyllic and majestic locations to hike, fish, camp, or enjoy the outdoors. I appreciate spending time outdoors myself, but as I get older it has become more challenging to hike, and instead, I take road trips across the Upper Peninsula and see sights that are accessible to the non-hiker.

This book is a list of locations I have visited on my travels around the UP along with tips I have learned along the way. I have had many people request a book specifically on traveling the Upper Peninsula. Some of the locations have been previously printed in my Lost In Michigan books, but there are also places that have not been published until now. Whether it's your first time to the UP or you have visited multiple times, I think you will find this book helpful in planning your first or next trip to Michigan's Upper Peninsula.

Contents

Tips and Advice

St Ignace Area

Sault Ste. Marie Area

Whitefish Point Area

Manistique Area

South Central Area

Pictured Rocks Area

Marquette Area

Huron Mountains

Keweenaw Area

Western UP

Tips and Advice

The Upper Peninsula is a unique and beautiful part of Michigan that attracts many visitors. The people who live there are known as Yoopers, referring to the initials UP. Tourists are known as "Trolls" because they live below or south of the big green bridge, which, of course, is the Mackinac Bridge.

The UP has many natural and man-made wonders that draw several trolls (tourists) to it, but for first time visitors, it can be a little overwhelming trying to decide what to see and where to stay. With my experience traveling and exploring the Upper Peninsula for www.lostinmichigan.net, I want to share some of the things I have learned. I am not going to give you specific places to stay and eat because everyone's tastes and needs are different, but I want to share with you some advice to help you choose your destinations in the UP.

Traveling

The UP is a lot larger than most people think it is. If you want to see the Soo Locks and the Lake of the Clouds in the Porcupine Mountains, be aware that it is about 270 miles and a five-hour drive between them, and that is if you don't stop to see any sites along the way. If you decide to go to Tahquamenon Falls, that can easily add a couple of hours to the trip. I suggest if you are only going to be in the UP for a few days to pick a region to visit and not try to see everything listed in the travel brochures all at once, especially if you have young kids. They will get bored riding in the car for a long trip between destinations.

Make sure you have a paper map or an atlas with you. Do not rely on your GPS because it thinks that an old overgrown logging trail is a road and will route you down it. Or it may take you down a road through the woods only to hit a gate for private property that you cannot cross. If you use your phone for a map or GPS, the signal may be weak when you need it, and all you get is a circle spinning as it tries to load a map. Sure, you can use GPS for navigating, but if you think it is taking you somewhere it shouldn't, trust your gut and ignore it, and take a route on the main roads if possible.

If you are traveling around the Upper Peninsula for any length of time, it is inevitable that at some point you will need a bathroom break. Below the bridge you can usually find a rest area or fast food restaurant for a place to use the bathroom. In the UP, the most common places outside of large cities are roadside parks or rustic campgrounds. Most do not have electricity or running water, so the facility is usually an outhouse. They go by many names such as pit toilet or vault toilet, but whatever you want to call them they are not the most enjoyable place to visit, but if you want an adventure, that is part of it. My recommendation is to carry toilet paper and hand sanitizer with you just in case you need it and the outhouse does not have it.

Anyone who has lived in Michigan for a while knows there are basically two seasons. Winter and road construction season. As soon as the snow melts, the orange barrels come out, and the UP is no exception. MDOT and the county road commissions have to keep up on the maintenance of the roads across the Upper Peninsula. It may not be as prevalent as it is in the big cities such as the Detroit Metro Area; it is different in the UP In the big cities, a two lane road may be choked down to one lane. In the Upper Peninsula, most roads are only one lane in either direction. Most likely there will be a flag person stopping traffic in one direction. Just be patient and wait because more than likely any road detouring around it could end up being a two-track road through the forests or a bumpy washboarded dirt road.

Food

Finding a place to eat can be a lot different than what you are used to. If you live downstate in the southern part of Michigan, you have a large number of choices from fast food to chain restaurants and local mom and pop diners. Some of the large cities have popular chain restaurants and fast food franchises. If you are planning on stopping at restaurants when you are hungry in the UP, it will be mostly locally owned places. Most that I have eaten at have been good with some being excellent that I visit on almost every trip to the UP. Because cell phone Internet can be spotty, I recommend doing some research beforehand on places where you want to dine at. I also pack stuff for a picnic in case I get hungry and am a long distance away from any towns. You can usually find a roadside park, and many popular tourist spots have areas or parks with picnic tables.

Yoopers also have some unique food that is mostly found in the Upper Peninsula. They love their pasties, which are like a meat and potatoes pie. There are many roadside stands and restaurants that sell them. One thing to know is Yoopers like them plain or with ketchup. Sometimes they offer gravy, but that is their way of knowing you are a troll if you accept their offer of "troll sauce". Cudighi sandwiches (pronounced cut-a-gee) are also popular in bars and restaurants throughout the

UP. They are an Italian sausage patty cooked on a flat top served on Italian bread with marinara sauce. The UP being surrounded by Lake Michigan and Lake Superior, fish is especially popular at most restaurants. You will also find a lot of smoked fish at gas stations and party stores.

You are on a UP adventure, and you should try new and different places and things to eat. You never know that a small town bar or roadside stand could have the best food you have ever eaten.

Lodging

Other than a few major cities, you will not find a lot of large chain hotels. You will see a lot of small mom and pop motels. I have found most of them to be a nice place to stay, but you need to do your research as some are not as nice. In my experience, I have met some really nice people who are owner operators of small hotels.

Camping is another good option for a place to stay on your visit. State parks are a good option and are extremely popular; you need to make reservations well in advance. If you don't have any camping equipment, they have some cabins you can rent. If you like to camp, don't forget to check the local city and county campgrounds. They have some nice full hookup sites that you may find useful if you have a travel trailer or RV.

The state and national forest campgrounds may be a good option if you like to rough it in a tent since they usually do not offer electricity or running water. Most have a fee that is paid by the honor system. There is usually a post with envelopes for you to deposit a fee. I like to have a variety of cash in multiple increments so I can pay the fee. It seems like they are always an odd number like 16 or 17 dollars. You don't want to be stuck with only twenty dollar bills or debit cards. I will even go old school and take my checkbook so I can write a check if I need to. Wherever you camp, be sure to bring some bug spray as the mosquitoes can and most likely will be out in full force.

Bugs and Insects

If you visit the Upper Peninsula in the summertime bugs and insects are something that you are going to have to deal with. If you are camping or hiking in the woods, you are definitely going to want some bug repellent or the mosquitoes will eat you alive. You also have to be on the lookout for ticks on your clothes, legs and arms if you are out hiking.

The months of May and June are the height of black fly season, but they can be out anytime during the summer months. They are black flies that bite exposed skin and can be extremely painful, almost like being stung. Long sleeve shirts and pants can help to keep the biting flies away, but they can get annoying when you are on the beach suntanning or swimming.

Bugs can also be a nuisance when you are driving. Especially at night in swampy areas. It sounds like rain pelting your windshield, but it's actually insects, and the bug guts can be annoying to look through on a long road trip. I have been taking along a roll of paper towels and some window cleaner just to clean my windshield between stops at the gas station.

Don't let the bugs keep you from exploring the Upper Peninsula. Just be prepared for them, and you will enjoy your trip even more.

Saint Ignace Area

The Mackinac Bridge

Location:
I-75 Across the Straits of
Mackinac between Mackinaw
City and St. Ignace

If you live west of Michigan you will probably enter the
Upper Peninsula through Wisconsin but if you are a
Michigander you will go across the Mackinac Bridge at the tip
of the mitten. It is a five-mile-long bridge, and the view is

spectacular. The center lanes of the bridge have a grate which can be a little interesting to drive on as your vehicle will sometimes shift side to side as you go from one grate to the next. Some people have anxiety about driving over the bridge especially if it is their first time. The speed on the bridge is 45 miles an hour, so if you just obey the speed limit and take your time, it can be a fun trip across one of the largest bridges in the world.

There is a $4 toll to cross the bridge. I recommend you keep $4 easily accessible in your vehicle if you know you're going to be crossing it so when you stop to pay your toll you are not fumbling around for money to give to the attendant. In my experience, the booths in the left lane tend to move faster and the lines are shorter than the right lanes. I think people prefer the right lane because immediately after the toll booths is a Welcome Center that has restrooms and travel information. The Welcome Center is a wonderful place to stop and get brochures and maps for your adventure through the UP.

St Ignace

St. Anthony's Rock

St Anthony's Rock
Near 55 Central Hill
St Ignace, MI 49781
45.86795394929193,
-84.72636178292396

Wawatam Lighthouse
Near 251 S. N State St.
St Ignace, MI 49781
45.866017473314585,
-84.71548622575351

Castle Rock
N2690 Castle Rock Rd.
St Ignace, MI 49781
45.91069842717006,
-84.74159280178588

The town of St Ignace sits at the northern end of the Mackinac Bridge and is one of the oldest cities in the nation. It is a popular stop for travelers since it has many restaurants and gift shops downtown along with ferries that take visitors to

Mackinac Island. Behind the gift shops on Main Street in the parking lot is a strange rock formation known as St Anthony's Rock. It was used by early sailors as a landmark in the early days of the town.

Wawatam Lighthouse

The Wawatam Lighthouse that stands on the pier in town is one of Michigan's most recent lighthouses. Originally, it stood at a Welcome Center in Monroe Michigan but was moved to St Ignace and now stands as an aid to navigation and watches the ferries pass by. It is named after the Chief Wawatam ferry that crossed the straits before the bridge was constructed. You can see remnants of the dock near the lighthouse.

If you take the main road, which is US-2, north through town where it connects back in with I-75, you'll find Castle Rock. It's kind of a tourist trap, but it has a nice gift shop, and for a few dollars you can climb the stairs to the top of Castle Rock. If you're older like me, it is a little bit of a hike, and you may have to stop and catch your breath a few times, but the view is worth it.

Bridge View Park

W69 Boulevard Dr, St Ignace, MI 49781
45.846638144964956, -84.72604661382746

Bridge View Park sits next to I-75 on the west side of the bridge on the Lake Michigan shoreline. It can be accessed either from an exit next to the toll booths on I-75 or from Boulevard Drive off US-2 near the on ramp for I-75. It has a great view of the bridge, especially in the evening when the sun is shining on it from the west. The park also has a newly built restroom building and information about the history and constructions of the bridge. Outside is a memorial to the workers who died while constructing the bridge. A bell is on display that once stood in the south tower and used as a fog signal for passing ships.

Gros Cap Cemetery

1502 U.S. Rte 2
St Ignace, MI 49781
45.869284976466055,
-84.79934229793123

About three miles west of St. Ignace along US-2 is the Gros Cap Cemetery. It is one of the oldest continuously operated cemeteries in the United States. In the 1600s, a large group of Ottawa Indians settled in the area and established a burial ground, which is now part of the present day cemetery. Over the centuries, both Native Americans and European settlers have been laid to rest in the cemetery. A wide variety of headstones and grave markers can be seen in this pretty little graveyard. From wooden crosses to modern granite marks, it spans a lot of history. I wonder how many people just pass by without knowing the history of this cemetery.

The Mystery Spot

N916 Martin Lake Rd.
St Ignace, MI 49781
45.87424926973405,
-84.808749190139

You will see many signs and billboards for the Mystery Spot. It has been a roadside tourist trap since the 1950s, and I think everyone should visit it at least once in their life. Without giving away the secret, the main attraction is a cabin with optical illusions that defy gravity. It also has a zip line, miniature golf and a maze. It is an "old school" attraction that harkens back to a time of the late 1900s when families traveled to northern Michigan in their station wagons to see America after World War II. It also has a nice gift shop if you want to stop and check it out before you pay for a tour.

U.S.-2 Lake Michigan Beach

4319-2947, U.S. Rte 2
Moran, MI 49760
45.93422631633661,
-84.91892903319047

About ten miles west of St Ignace US-2 travels along next to the shoreline of Lake Michigan. It is about a two-mile long stretch of sandy beach and a popular stop on a hot summer day. Parallel parking is along the east bound or southern side of US-2. It is a great spot if you have an RV, your door and awning will face the beach. It is extremely popular in summer and can be difficult to find a spot to park, so I recommend getting there in the morning if you plan on visiting this beach.

Cut River Bridge

U.S. Rte 2 Between
Brevort and Epouffet
46.04508842913419,
-85.12527115410748

The Cut River Bridge on US-2 passes over the Cut River, which has carved a gorge into the landscape over the several centuries it has flowed into Lake Michigan. From the topside, it seems like most bridges, but if you stop at the rest area next to the bridge, you can walk down underneath it and see the myriad of green steel girders.

19

It's near the town of Epoufette about 25 miles west of St. Ignace. Construction of the bridge began in 1941 but was halted during WWII. The 641-foot-long bridge was finally completed in 1947. Under the east end of the bridge is a wooden door in the stone foundation. A brass plate on the door reads "T. Troll". I am not sure if it is the Troll's office or home, but whenever I knocked, Mr. Troll never answered. It is a good place to stop and stretch your legs and take a bathroom break, but be warned it is an outhouse and it gets a lot of use.

Fiborn Quarry

Parking located off Fiborn
Quarry Road about five
miles north of Trout Lake
Road.
46.207291794672486,
-85.1691679958276

Hidden in the woods in the central-eastern Upper Peninsula
not far from Trout Lake are the remnants of the old Fiborn
Quarry. At its peak, the Fiborn Limestone Co. had two
locomotives and a small town of 75 people who worked for
the quarry. It operated until the 1930s, when the depression
crippled the company's ability to operate. The ruins of some
of the buildings are now part of the Karst Preserve which lies
between St. Ignace and Newberry. It is about a mile hike to the
ruins but worth the walk to see the ruins of some old historic
buildings.

Hessel

Along the Lake Michigan
shoreline off M-134
46.0040994021111,
-84.42793044575508

The town of Hessel sits along Lake Huron about thirty miles east of St. Ignace. It is an historic harbor town and is known for its annual vintage wooden boat show the second weekend in August. One of my favorite stops during the summer is the E. J. Mertaugh Boat Works. It is a working marina and boat repair facility, but the store has an excellent ice cream shop that serves Michigan-made Moomers ice cream. The township park on the shoreline has an excellent beach for relaxing in the sun. The town is also home to Our Lady of the Snows Catholic Church. It is a unique looking church building, and next to it is a Native American cemetery.

Drummond Island

Drummond Island Ferry
113 Huron St, De Tour
Village, MI 49725
45.992886465316644,
-83.89838281176529

Drummond Island Is one of the largest islands in the Great
Lakes and sits in Lake Huron off the eastern tip of the Upper
Peninsula. A fifteen-minute ferry ride from De Tour Village
transports vehicles to the island. The island is a wonderful
place for hiking and camping, and its biggest draw is the ORV
trails. It has sixty miles of ATV trails and forty miles of full
size vehicle trails popular with Jeepers. During the fall season it
is a popular hunting location.

Sault Ste. Marie Area

Sault Ste. Marie

Chippewa County Courthouse

Chippewa County Courthouse
319 Court St,
Sault Ste. Marie, MI 49783

Lake Superior State University
Ryan Ave.
Sault Ste. Marie, MI 49783

Museum Ship Valley Camp
501 E. Water St.
Sault Ste. Marie, MI 49783

Sault Ste Marie is mostly known for the Soo Locks. It is where enormous great lakes freighters are raised or lowered to match up with the difference in water levels between Lake Huron and Lake Superior. The locks are downtown, and visitors can watch the ships pass through them. I recommend installing a marine traffic app on your phone so you can track the ships as they pass through the locks. Across from the locks are a row of gift shops, restaurants and fudge shops and it is a popular place for tourists. If you are enthralled by the massive freighters that travel the Great Lakes and you have always wanted to see what they look like inside, then you need to check out the *SS Valley Camp*. The 550-foot-long ship was launched in 1917 and sailed until the 1980s, when it was permanently moored in Sault Ste Marie and converted into a museum ship.

Fort Brady Officer Housing now part of LSSU

West of town is Lake Superior State College. During the summer months, most of the students are gone, but it is interesting to walk around the campus. Before it was a college it was Fort Brady, built by the military in the late 1800s. If you love old historic architecture, be sure to visit the Chippewa County Courthouse. It is one of the oldest courthouses in Michigan, and the stone and brickwork is amazing.

If you love to camp, Aune Osborn Campground is right on the St Mary's River. It is managed by the city of Sault Ste. Marie, and if you are lucky, you can get a campsite right next to the water. The ships make their turn in the river and sail close to the shoreline.

Sugar Island

Sugar Island Ferry
near 1425 Riverside Dr,
Sault Ste. Marie, MI 49783
46.486152853774044,
-84.30208282054791

Church of Our Saviour
10189 E Northshore Dr.
Sault Ste. Marie, MI 49783
46.52756435256712,
-84.15131772406653

Finn Hall
Corner Of
E. 6-1/2 Mile Road and
S. Homestead Rd.
46.412594695247805,
-84.20719645891481

East of Sault Ste. Marie next to Aune Osborn Campground is the car ferry to Sugar Island. It is about a five-minute ride across the St. Mary's River to the Island. It is a large island—about five miles across and ten miles long. It is mostly farmland and summer cottages but does have a few interesting historical sites.

Church of Our Saviour

At the north end of the island is an old church started by Bishop Baraga in 1853. Church of Our Saviour, Friend of Children, also known as Holy Angels Roman Catholic Church, is a cute little wooden church and makes for a nice photo opportunity. It was used continuously until 1953, when it was closed. In 1982, it was reopened and used for an annual Mass to celebrate Bishop Baraga's birthday. If you are into old cemeteries, behind the church is Payment Cemetery, named after Michael Payment, who started a settlement in the area and donated the land for the church and cemetery. It was a somewhat difficult hike up a rocky path, and I imagine it would be challenging to get landscaping equipment back there. The cemetery has a lot of tall grass and ferns growing among the tombstones and wooden crosses marking the graves of people laid to rest decades ago.

Near the center of the Island is Finn Hall. It was built in 1925 by Finnish immigrants using locally grown and milled lumber. The hall has been renovated by the Sugar Island Historical Preservation Society. Other than driving around and exploring the island, there is not a lot to do on the island, but if you have never ridden in your vehicle on a car ferry, it can be a lot of fun, especially if you have young children.

Brimley State Park

9200 W 6 Mile Rd.
Brimley, MI 49715
46.48065947108821,
-84.52914951652002

Brimley State Park is about ten miles west of Sault Ste. Marie and sits along the shoreline of Lake Superior. It has about two hundred campsites and newly constructed bathroom buildings. It is an excellent place to stay if you enjoy camping. It is located between the Soo and Whitefish Point and is situated nearby several sites to visit and works well as a base camp if you want to stay there for a week. It is also close to stores such as Meijers or Walmart. The park also offers a wonderful beach on Lake Superior. It is open for day visitors, and is a great place to cool off on a hot day and watch the ships sailing through the locks.

The town of Brimley is a nice little town to stop for some snacks and gas for a drive up the shoreline to Whitefish Point. The town has a few restaurants and a nice bakery along with a small grocery store.

Bay Mills and Mission

Native American Cemetery
12190 W Lakeshore Dr.
Brimley, MI 49715
46.45359485418309,
-84.60502461652483

Bay Mills is known for its casino, but along the road is an old Native American cemetery, and according to the sign in the back, it was established in 1841. The graves are covered with wooden spirit houses. The wooden houses are built to protect the body as the soul passes to the spirit world. Many times relatives would leave food and tools for the deceased loved one to use as they travel to the spirit world. The cemetery is not open to the public, but it is next to the road and visible to motorists.

Mission Hill

Mission Hill Overlook
W. Tower Rd.
Brimley, MI 49715
46.4587609328394,
-84.63851115970904

West of the casino and community college on W. Lakeshore Drive is Tower Road. It forks off to the south, and if you take that road for about a half mile, it will turn and take you to Mission Hill. At the top is an overlook with a spectacular view of Spectacle Lake, Point Iroquois Lighthouse and Lake Superior.

At the top of the hill is Mission Hill Cemetery, an old historic cemetery with a white picket fence in the middle of it. Buried inside are the remains of eight crew members of the *S.S. Myron*. The steamer sank in a storm in November 1919 near Whitefish Point. The crew escaped in lifeboats but unfortunately, the little boats did not save their lives. Eight bodies were found onshore encased in ice in the spring of 1920. The crewmen were buried in Mission Hill Cemetery, spending eternity together. The captain who stayed with the ship was saved while floating on a piece of wreckage.

Dollar Settlement

Intersection of
W. Lakeshore Drive and
S. Ranger Rd.
46.460628955983566,
-84.73904189302739

Traveling down the W. Lakeshore Drive that follows the Lake Superior shoreline, you will come across an old Pullman car. According to the map, the town is—or at least was—Dollar Settlement. I could not find any info about this sparsely populated town. The old railroad car was brought in to be converted into a diner, but it never materialized. Now it just sits in Dollar Settlement watching tourists pass by. It is on private property and not accessible to tourists, but it is interesting to see it sitting there miles away from any railroad tracks.

Robert Dollar was the founder of Dollarville near Newberry, and he built a dock on Lake Superior for his sawmill and lumber company. I am guessing that is where Dollar Settlement got its name from, but I have never been able to confirm it.

Point Iroquois Lighthouse

12942 W. Lakeshore Drive
Brimley, MI 49715
46.484297477833685,
-84.63209344495112

When Congress approved the funding for the Soo Locks in 1853, they also set aside money for the construction of a lighthouse on Point Iroquois to guide ships into the mouth of the St. Mary's River. The first lighthouse was built of stone and rubble with a wooden lantern deck, and stood only forty-five feet tall. About ten years after its construction, government inspectors began to question the integrity of the structure. In 1870, the first lighthouse was razed, and a two-story lighthouse with a sixty-five-foot-tall tower was constructed. In 1905, an addition was added for another assistant keeper. A head lighthouse keeper and two assistants maintained the light and fog horn.

The station was deactivated in 1962, replaced by the Canadian-operated Gros Cap Reefs Light, an unmanned buoy-type beacon in the St. Mary's River Channel. In 1963, the original lens was sent to the Smithsonian Institution. Currently, the lighthouse is a museum, and visitors can climb the stairs to the top of the tower. Although the light is gone, the view is spectacular. When the museum is closed, check the stairs to the tower. Sometimes the door is open for visitors to climb the tower for a small donation in the box near the door.

Naomikong Bridge

Naomikong Overlook
Lake Superior Shoreline Rd.
Eckerman, MI 49728
46.473792495577804,
-84.95724594702395

Naomikong Bridge Location
46.47628315817264,
-84.97010935566612

About fifteen miles west of Point Iroquois Lighthouse is Naomikong Creek. Near the bridge that crosses over the creek on W. Lakeshore Drive is the Naomikong Overlook parking lot. There you will find a trail that leads down to the

Naomikong Bridge. The bridge is a wooden suspension bridge and is known as "the Mini Mac". It is part of the four thousand mile long North Country National Scenic Hiking Trail that takes hikers from North Dakota to Vermont.

Camp Raco

USFS 3154 south off M-28
46.36736785429408,
-84.73887799891777

Hidden in the National Forest in the Upper Peninsula among the trees is an old stone chimney not far from M-28 in Brimley Township. It's the remains of Camp Raco, Michigan's first Civilian Conservation Corps (CCC) facility. The camp was created in 1933 by President Roosevelt's New Deal plan. Two hundred young men from Detroit built the camp and lived there while working on conservation projects in the UP. They built roads, and planted trees and buildings for public use.

The camp closed in 1942 but was opened back up during World War II and used as a prisoner of war camp. It housed 267 German Nazis captured by the allied forces. After the war, the buildings were removed, and only the foundations and the chimney remain. You can find it on M-28 by looking for the small wooden National Forest sign for Camp Raco.

Whitefish Point Area

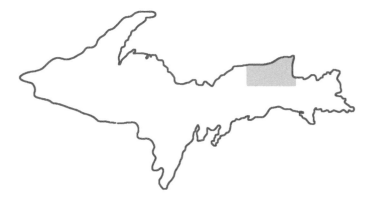

Tahquamenon Falls

Upper Tahquamenon Falls

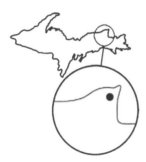

Tahquamenon Falls State Park
41382 W. M-123
Paradise, MI 49768

Lower Falls
46.60449326905391,
-85.20886256483064

Upper Falls
46.57626474650513,
-85.2565028510891

44

Tahquamenon Falls State Park is one of the busiest locations in the summer and autumn in the Upper Peninsula. Located north of Newberry near Paradise, the park's main attraction, is the Upper and Lower Tahquamenon Falls. The falls get extremely busy with cars lined up to enter the park. I recommend trying to get there in the morning to beat the afternoon crowds.

The upper falls are one of the largest waterfalls east of the Mississippi River and drop about fifty feet. It is a short walk from the parking lot to the stairs that lead to the top of the falls. It is about ninety steps to the top of the falls and another one hundred ten steps to the river below. The upper falls has a brewery and restaurant if you want to take a break for lunch.

The lower falls are not as tall as the upper, but there are not a lot of stairs to view them. A boardwalk leads along the river's edge to the many cascades and drops. A newly constructed bridge leads to the island that was previously only accessible by renting a rowboat. The gift shop at the lower falls is also a great place for an ice cream cone on a hot day.

Lower Tahquamenon Falls

If you enjoy hiking, the park has many hiking trails, and one trail will take you from the upper to the lower falls.

During the winter months, the lower falls are closed to vehicle traffic and only accessible by snowshoeing or cross country skiing. The upper falls are open in the winter, and if you are not afraid of the cold, they are worth checking out when covered in snow and ice. There are also a lot less visitors during the winter.

Crisp Point Lighthouse

1944 Co Hwy 412
Newberry, MI 49868
46.75307270954636,
-85.25746439571108

Crisp Point Lighthouse is the "other light" on the Upper Peninsula's Whitefish Point. The Whitefish Point Lighthouse, north of Paradise, is rather easy to get to, but the Crisp Point lighthouse is about twenty miles of dirt road through the dense Upper Peninsula forest. If you have ever run a 5K road race or maybe climbed Mt. Everest, you know that just completing the feat is an accomplishment. It's kind of the same thing for the Crisp Point Lighthouse. Just getting to the lighthouse is an achievement.

The coastline of Lake Superior between Whitefish Point and Grand Marais has always been treacherous for passing ships. Sailors gave it the nickname "Shipwreck Coast" because of all the shipwrecks. The U.S. Lifesaving Service established a life-saving station at the point in 1876 to rescue sailors caught in Mother Nature's fury. The second station keeper was Christopher Crisp, and the point and lifesaving station were referred to as Crisp's Point. Eventually, it was just called Crisp Point. A decision was made that a lighthouse was needed to warn captains of the danger off Crisp Point and to help them navigate the dangerous waters. In 1903, the lighthouse was built with an attached service room that still stands today. A two-story keeper's dwelling and a second assistant keeper's dwelling were built, along with a fog-signal building. An electric illuminated buoy was placed offshore notifying captains of the turn into Whitefish Bay. The lighthouse and lifesaving station were decommissioned, and all the buildings were razed except the lighthouse tower.

In 1988, Don and Nellie Ross from Ohio found the abandoned lighthouse. They fell in love with the old tower so much that they moved to the Upper Peninsula and formed the Crisp Point Light Historical Society to save the remaining structure. Lake Superior eroded the shoreline to the edge of the abandoned lighthouse, and a storm in 1992 destroyed the service room, leaving only the foundation. The service room was reconstructed in 2006, and a visitors center was built in 2009. The society continues to maintain the lighthouse and welcomes visitors in the summer months.

The fun part is getting to the lighthouse. In the 1930s, one of the men stationed at the lighthouse wrote in his journal that he traveled as far as he could by car and then hiked by snowshoe another twenty miles to the lighthouse. In the present day, you don't have to hike, but it is a fun and challenging journey by car.

To get to the lighthouse, go west past Tahquamenon State Park on M-123 then turn north on County Road 500, which isn't that bad of road for a dirt road. But then you get to County Road 412, which is a seasonal road, and that road is a winding, twisting path through the woods. The way to the lighthouse is marked with small wooden signs at the intersections. Also be aware that you will not have any cell phone service along the way, as you are in no-man's land in the Upper Peninsula.

I was heading down the road, fording the water holes, getting deeper and deeper into the wilderness where cell service is non-existent. It left me without voice, text or internet on my phone out in the middle of Whitefish Point. I arrived at a spot in my journey where a sign on the side of the road marks the location where two sisters were stranded for thirteen days in their SUV in April 2015. I hoped I wouldn't have any breakdowns or anything. Signs are posted about every mile to let visitors know there is an emergency telephone at the lighthouse. The signs must have been added after the sisters got stranded.

It took me an hour to get from the lighthouse to Tahquamenon Falls, but it was well worth the trip. If you have the time to do it, I would highly recommend it, but make sure you have a reliable car (or better yet, a truck or SUV) and plenty of gas. I burned about a quarter tank getting there and back, and I would also make sure to have some water and food, just in case.

Newberry

Luce County Sheriff's Residence

Historical Museum and former
Sheriff's residence
407 W Harrie St.
Newberry, MI 49868
46.352428265327084,
-85.51527990978641

The town of Newberry is the largest city in the Whitefish
Point Region. It has a grocery store, hardware store, hospital
and repair facilities. Hopefully, you don't need your car
repaired or a hospital, but you will find them in Newberry. It

also has some larger hotels and fast food, but there are a lot of family-owned restaurants and lodges in Newberry for you to try when you are in town.

One of the more interesting places in town is the old Luce County Jail and Sheriff's residence. It was built in 1894. The Luce County Historical Society rescued this building from demolition in 1975 and restored it as the Luce County Historical Museum in 1976.

If you are heading into town from the south on M-123 you will probably notice the razor wire fences surrounding the Newberry Correctional Facility. The property started out as the Upper Peninsula Asylum for the Insane. If you drive down the road next to the prison, you will see some of the old structures from the hospital. They are next to the prison, so do not go poking around them, but they are interesting to see from the road.

Two Hearted River

Near 32752 Co Rd 423
Newberry, MI 49868
46.6990416282773,
-85.42262194465445

Two Hearted River flows into Lake Superior west of the Crisp Point Lighthouse. Near the mouth of the river is a one of a kind suspension bridge with wood planking for hikers to cross. The bridge is located in the state forest campground and leads over to a sandy beach with rocks along the shoreline. It is a great place to enjoy the refreshing water of Lake Superior or go rock hunting for your favorite rocks. The bridge is also part of the North Country Trail that runs from North Dakota to Vermont and passes through Michigan.

I recommend taking Road 414 over to 423 and then head north to the mouth of the river. Do not trust your GPS since it will take you down forest trails only drivable by ATVs and dirt bikes.

Whitefish Point Lighthouse

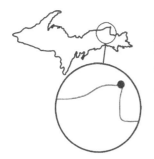

18335 N Whitefish Point Rd.
Paradise, MI 49768
46.77142454329075,
-84.95796710309081

This is the oldest lighthouse on Lake Superior and began operating in 1849. The point marks the course change for ore boats and other ships navigating this treacherous coastline to and from St. Mary's Canal. Since 1971, the light, fog signal, and radio beacon have been automated and controlled from Sault Ste. Marie. It has a unique steel tube light tower to withstand the gale force winds that blow during storms on Lake Superior.

The lighthouse and other buildings are now used as the Great Lakes Shipwreck Museum. It has many artifacts from the *Edmund Fitzgerald* that sank off Whitefish Point during a storm in 1976. If you visit this historic lighthouse, be sure to walk down to the lake. It is a great spot for rock hunters to find their favorite stone.

Paradise

 M-123 near the Lake Superior Shoreline
46.627386643087554,
-85.03745596792207

The small town of Paradise is the heart of Whitefish Point. It is centrally located between the lighthouse at the point and the Tahquamenon Falls State Park. It is a great place to stop and get gas or food for your next adventure. You can pick up supplies for a picnic or eat at one of the restaurants or bars in the town. It's also a good place to check your phone for texts from your family back home or you can send them a text to make them jealous. I would do it in Paradise because cell service in most of Whitefish Point is non-existent.

Vermillion Point

N Vermillion Rd.
Paradise, MI 49768
46.763143870652485,
-85.15192307170359

Before it was incorporated into the Coast Guard, the U.S. Lifesaving Service rescued sailors in peril on the Great Lakes. The unofficial motto of the U.S. Lifesaving Service was "You have to go out; you don't have to come back." Of all the stations in Michigan, Vermilion Point was the most remote and desolate. Located on the shores of Lake Superior near Whitefish Point, the station was situated between Crisp Point Lighthouse and Whitefish Point Lighthouse. The remote outpost was called "the Alcatraz of the Lifesaving Service" by the men and their families stationed there.

The station began operation in 1876. Due to its remote location, supplies were sent by boat during the shipping season. In the wintertime, supplies had to be delivered by dog sled because of the deep snow. The station remained in operation until 1944 when it was abandoned. The buildings were left alone to defend themselves from the harsh northern Michigan weather. In the early 1970s, the Vermilion Life Saving Station and surrounding 1.5 miles of undeveloped shoreline were privately purchased. The old station was donated to Lake Superior State University for educational and research purposes. In the mid 90s, the university returned the property to the private owner. The Little Traverse Conservancy eventually acquired the land and former life-saving station buildings. The conservancy manages the land and has a partnership with the non-profit group S.O.S. (Save Our Station) Vermilion, who works on saving and restoring the buildings.

The property is open to the public for quiet recreation. The areas around the piping plover nests and bird-trapping nets are restricted, but there is access to the Lake Superior shoreline. Visitors can also walk the grounds of the old Life Saving Station. The buildings are not open to the public, but you can look through the windows to get a feel for life at this remote Upper Peninsula location.

It is about a ten-mile drive down sandy forest roads from N. Whitefish Point Road to reach Vermilion Point. It's worth the trip if you are in the area, but I suggest doing it in the summer or fall when it is dry. The first trip I made to the point, the road was flooded over about a mile from the parking lot and I had to turn around.

Muskellunge Lake

29881 Co. Rd. 407
Newberry, MI 49868
46.679039309713936,
-85.62781855853389

Muskellunge Lake is about twenty-five miles north of Newberry and sits near Lake Superior. It is a large lake with crystal clear water and popular with fishermen, and the Muskellunge State Park is popular with campers and ORV riders. It is one of the few state parks that allow ATVs to be operated in the park but only from your site to the nearby trails. It is a wonderful park to visit if you are not camping there. It has a beach on both Muskellunge Lake and Lake Superior. There is a day use parking lot near the access to Lake Superior, and if you like rock hunting, it is an excellent beach to look for stones washed up on the beach. If the water of Lake Superior is cold, you can go to the nice sandy beach in the campground on Muskellunge Lake.

The entrance to the park is on Deer Park Road. If you take it to the west, it will connect to the Grand Marais Truck Trail. It does not look like a long distance on the map to Grand Marais, but be warned that the dirt roads get a lot of ORV use and are washboarded and rough, and you will need to go slow. They can also be dusty in the summer or muddy in the spring and fall. It is a nice trip along Lake Superior—just plan on driving slower than you would expect.

Manistique Area

Manistique

Water Tower
Deer St.
Manistique, MI 49854
45.962894168236865,
-86.25051282531992

Located along the shore of Lake Michigan on US-2, Manistique is an excellent place to stop for a break while exploring the Upper Peninsula. You can relax at its waterfront park or take a stroll downtown. When you are in Manistique, you may notice a strange-looking brick tower north of downtown. After running out of water to fight a fire in the early 1900s, it was evident that the town's water system needed to be upgraded. A pumping station and water tower were constructed near the Manistique River. I am not sure why the community of Manistique chose to build the tower the way they did, but it is one of the most unique water towers in the country. An ornate Roman Revival style design was chosen to hold the two hundred thousand gallon tank. The tower was constructed in 1922 from bricks, and a copper dome roof sits atop the 137-foot-tall tower. This unique tower provided water to the city until 1954, when the wooden pipes used to collect water from the river began to fail. A new system was built, and the elaborate tower was no longer needed. It was used for offices until the Schoolcraft Historical Society obtained the historic tower. Along with other buildings on the property, the society runs it as a museum for visitors.

If you visit the tower you will travel over the world famous Siphon Bridge. I say "world famous" because the bridge was featured in Ripley's Believe It Or Not, as it was the only bridge in the world with the road deck lower than the water level of the river. The local paper mill needed more water so the level of the Manistique River was raised. The sides of the bridge are made of solid concrete, allowing the water level to rise up the sides of the bridge. The paper mill closed some time ago and the water level has been lowered to its normal level making the bridge just an ordinary river crossing.

Fayette

4785 II Rd.
Garden, MI 49835
45.71891764236024,
-86.6703770807702

The historic and dormant town of Fayette is in the Garden Peninsula, which juts out into Lake Michigan along the southern part of the UP Fayette is about twenty miles south of US-2. The town, which is now part of the Fayette Historic State Park, was started by Jackson Iron Company in 1867. After the Civil War, iron and steel were in high demand. The site, located in Snail Shell Harbor, was an ideal spot for an iron furnace and shipping harbor. The town was named after Fayette Brown, one of the company's directors.

In the late 1800s, the town grew to over five hundred residents, most of whom worked for the Jackson Iron Company. Workers smelted the iron ore in the town's furnace to produce pig iron, which was used to make steel. Pig iron was more efficient to ship than raw iron ore. The name pig iron comes from the shapes of the ingots in which the iron was poured. They looked like little piglets, so the name kinda stuck.

The town continued producing pig iron until the early 1890s. By that time, much of the timber used to fire the furnaces had been harvested. In addition to the dwindling firewood supply, more efficient methods of producing iron and steel had been created, and the town of Fayette was no longer profitable. Without any work, most of the residents left, and Fayette became more of a summer resort as people began enjoying the natural beauty surrounding the former iron smelting community. By the 1950s, the town had been purchased by the Escanaba Paper Company, which gave it to the Michigan government in exchange for timberland.

The historic town of Fayette is now part of Fayette State Park. It includes twenty buildings, of which nineteen are original. The buildings are open for visitors to tour and see what life was like in the early 1900s iron smelting town. It is more than just a side trip off US-2. It will take you about half an hour to get to Fayette from US-2, and when you do get there, give yourself at minimum of a couple of hours to walk around the town and explore all of the buildings.

Sac Bay

Sac Bay County Park
Located at the end of
8th Rd. Garden, MI 49835
45.656515980611154,
-86.70384288700394

Sac Bay is in the Garden Peninsula south of Fayette in the Upper Peninsula. It is a small bay on the shores of Big Bay De Noc, and a town of the same name was started in 1853. It was given a post office in 1860, but it was closed after a post office was opened in Fayette. This old building stands across from an old farm where the town once stood. It looks as if it was a general store at one time and then it had a metal addition added to it. There is a little county park along the bay, and it is a nice quiet place to visit if you are at Fayette.

Nahma

13747 Main St.
Nahma, MI 49864
45.840497198989006,
-86.66358202933806

The town of Nahma stands along the Lake Michigan shoreline in Big Bay De Noc east of Escanaba at the mouth of the Sturgeon River. The town got its name from the river and the fish that swam in it because Nahma is a Native American word for sturgeon.

The town was established in 1881 by the Bay de Noquet Lumber Company of Oconto, Wisconsin. At its peak, the company employed over 1500 people and built housing and stores for its employees. The company closed in 1951 and put the entire town up for sale, making national headlines. The unique opportunity to purchase a whole town was featured in several newspapers and also an article in Life magazine. An Indiana playground manufacturer purchased Nahma with the intention to convert the town into a resort community but never had the funding to do it. Eventually, the houses and buildings were sold off to individuals.

The town survives to this day and welcomes tourists who are enjoying the Upper Peninsula. It is about four miles south of US-2 and is a nice side trip when traveling across the UP. Tourists can visit the old general store or get a meal at the Nahma Inn. An old steam locomotive used by the sawmill stands on display in the park near the center of town.

The Christmas Tree Ship

US-2 east of Thompson
45.90680744806571,
-86.32455504933635

Along the Lake Michigan shoreline is a historical marker near the town of Thompson. It marks the spot where the "Christmas Tree Ship" sailed from with a load of pine trees for Chicago. One of the last shipping schooners to sail the Great Lakes was the *Rouse Simmons*. The three-masted schooner was built in 1868 to carry lumber. At the end of the sailing season, Captain Herman Schuenemann loaded the ship with Christmas trees from the Thompson forests and delivered them to the port of Chicago. Captain Schuenemann was known as Captain Santa and the *Rouse Simmons* had a pine tree tied to the top of the mast.

The *Rouse Simmons* left Thompson for Chicago on November 22, 1912. The ship sank in a late November snowstorm near Two Rivers Wisconsin. The captain and crew were never seen again. Captain Schuenemann's wife and daughters delivered trees to Chicago each Christmas until the 1930s.

Kitch-iti-kipi

Sawmill Rd
Manistique, MI 49854
46.005140294765404,
-86.38195821036345

Kitch-iti-kipi, sometimes referred to as Big Spring, is a natural wonder about ten miles northwest of Manistique. Located in Palms Book State Park, the spring feeds a pond that is about one hundred feet across. The state has built a large raft that can hold about fifty people.It is connected to a cable, and visitors can use a hand operated winch to move the raft across the pond. It has a canopy over the top and an opening in the center that you can look down into the crystal clear water. The view of the bubbling sands and fish swimming around is mesmerizing.

Ojibwe people who first lived in the area gave it the name Kitch-iti-kipi "Mirror of Heaven". Legend has it that a young chieftain died in the waters of the big spring when his canoe overturned while trying to impress a young woman. The water flows all year at 45 degrees and is an amazing sight in any time of year, including winter. During the summer months, the destination is extremely busy, and I recommend getting there early in the morning so you don't have to wait in line to ride on the raft.

Baraga's Chapel

Birch St.
Manistique, MI 49854
45.99475577978628,
-86.29380506558927

On the west side of Indian Lake is an old structure made of logs and bark. It was built in the 1980s to resemble a church built by Bishop Baraga. Frederick Baraga was called "The Apostle of the Ottawas and Chippewas". He was born and trained in Europe, and came to northern Michigan in the 1830s. He founded many missions in the northern Great Lakes Region, and the local Chippewas built a chapel on the shores of Indian Lake in 1832. The chapel was replaced by a larger one built the following year and stood until the 1870s. The chapel and other Native American structures stand in a shrine as a reminder of Baraga's early mission on the shores of Indian Lake.

Seul Choix Lighthouse

905 S. Seul Choix Pointe Road
Gulliver, MI 49840
45.9230343745498,
-85.91260304067131

Not far from US-2, near the town of Gulliver, between the "Bridge" and Escanaba, is Seul Choix Point Lighthouse. Seul Choix is a French word for "only choice" and is pronounced "sis shwa". It is one of the few harbors along the southern shore of the Upper Peninsula. That is how the name of the lighthouse came to be. It is still used as an active aid for navigation but also serves as a museum for visitors.

Stories claim the lighthouse is haunted by keeper Joseph Willie Townsend, who served at the structure from 1902 until his death in 1910. It is said that he passed away while in the bedroom that is located upstairs. Townsend and his wife lived in the lighthouse, and he was known to enjoy smoking cigars. Unfortunately, his wife was not a huge fan of the smell and smoke associated with the cigars, and forbade him to smoke in the house.

Since his death, many people have claimed to smell burning cigars in the house. It's believed that Townsend purposely smokes in the house in the afterlife as his wife can no longer stop him from doing it. People also claim to have seen Townsend's ghost and that furniture is rearranged. Another strange occurrence is that when the table is set for dinner with the forks facing up, if you leave to retrieve something and return to the table, sometimes the forks are facing down. Townsend was known to set his forks down in that position.

South Central Area

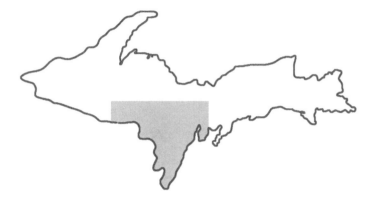

Peninsula Point Lighthouse

3722 County 513 T Rd.
Rapid River, MI 49878
45.67066724486545,
-86.96778188345692

The Stonington Peninsula juts into Lake Michigan from the southern coast of Michigan's Upper Peninsula separating Big and Little Bay De Noc. The lighthouse at the tip is known as Peninsula Point Lighthouse. It was constructed in 1865 after the Civil War and decommissioned in 1936. Tragically, the keeper's house that was attached to the tower burned in 1959. The tower was saved and is maintained by the National Forest Service. It's about an hour drive one way to the tower from US-2, and the last few miles are a winding two-track road through the dense forest, but it is well worth the trip to climb the tower for an amazing view of Lake Michigan.

In the early fall, you may get to witness one of nature's wonders. The monarch butterfly migrates 1,900 miles south to their wintering grounds in the Sierra Madre Mountains of Mexico. Usually, around September, thousands of monarchs gather around the remains of the old Peninsula Lighthouse at the tip of the Stonington Peninsula.

It is one of only a very few places in North America where monarchs can be viewed migrating in great numbers while they wait for favorable weather conditions. Since tagging began in the mid-1990s, monarchs tagged at Peninsula Point have been found in El Rosario, Mexico, almost 2,000 miles from the Stonington Peninsula. Monarchs use a combination of air currents and thermals to travel long distances. Some fly as far as 3,000 miles to reach their winter home.

Escanaba

Sand Point Lighthouse
2-20 Water Plant Rd.
Escanaba, MI 49829
45.74603820138121,
-87.0442535568825

Escanaba is the third largest city in the Upper Peninsula and the largest city on the Lake Michigan side. There you will find lodging, food, fuel or anything else you will need. The downtown has several historic buildings and shops, and the House of Ludington stands like a great white castle at the eastern end of downtown. They say the old building is haunted by friendly spirits. I am not sure about that, but entering the old building is like stepping back in time .

In Ludington Park is the beautifully restored Sand Point Lighthouse, and it marks the entrance to Little Bay De Noc. The strange thing about this lighthouse is that the tower faces away from the water, as if it were built backwards. In 1867, John Terry was appointed as the first lighthouse keeper during its construction. In 1868, he became ill and died before the dwelling was completed, and his wife Mary Terry was appointed to the position of Head Lightkeeper. Because of her husband's tragic death, she was one of the first female lighthouse keepers on the Great Lakes. Mary lit the Fresnel lens in the tower of the lighthouse for the first time on May 13,1868.

Mary and her late husband John did not have any children, and Mary lived alone in the lighthouse. She proudly fulfilled her duty as lightkeeper for several years until one winter night in 1886 when a fire broke out in the lighthouse, taking her life. The lighthouse was severely damaged, and no one knows what started the blaze. The rear door was forced open, and Mary was found on the floor in the oil-room, where fuel and supplies are stored for the lantern, instead of in bed, where she should have been sleeping, leaving some to speculate foul play was involved. Many people in the town of Escanaba knew Mary was careful and diligent in her duties of maintaining the lighthouse, and believed she was robbed and that the fire was set to destroy the evidence. I guess we will never know what happened to Mary or why the lighthouse was seemingly built "backwards", but it is a picturesque lighthouse to visit in Ludington Park.

Mansfield

Stream Road
Mansfield Township, MI 49920
46.11857896482249,
-88.22011482005838

Northeast of Crystal Falls along the river is a cute little log cabin church near the Michigamme River in the heart of the Upper Peninsula. The Mansfield Pioneer Church was in a small town that sprang up when ore was discovered in the area and mining began. Built in the late 1800s, it was the only church in Mansfield. It was maintained by a Lutheran Congregation but used by other faiths.

The mine started the little town but also upended the town because of its tragic end. The mine was dug under the Michigamme River, and miners claimed that they could hear the rushing water from the river above them. That did not stop the mine from expanding the shafts to extract ore until one tragic day. On September 28,1893, the mine collapsed, and the water from the river rushed in, drowning twenty-seven men. Their bodies were never recovered and have been entombed under the river for eternity.

When mining ended, the town's population dwindled. The church was used as a shingle mill and later fell into ruin. In the 1970s, a group of citizens formed a non-profit organization that restored the little church and continues to preserve the history of the area for travelers to visit. Visitors can step inside the church and sign the guest book. Down the road from the church is a monument to the miners who died when the mine collapsed.

Norway Spring

U.S. Rte 2, Norway, MI 49870
About one mile west of Norway
45.79668867267725,
-87.92696596301312

The town of Norway sits along US-2, and west of town next to the highway is a stone fountain. The water comes from an artesian spring and flows all year long. In 1903, Oliver Mining Company was searching for iron ore and drilled a hole about a thousand feet deep. The hole cuts several steeply dipping porous strata that trap water at higher elevations to the north. The difference in elevation creates the pressure in an artesian well. The back side of the fountain is a pipe with flowing water for filling up jugs. I stopped along my journey and filled up an empty water bottle that I had in my Jeep. I gotta say it is the best tasting water that I have ever had. If you are ever passing through Norway, be sure to bring a few jugs to fill up with water.

IXL Hermansville

5551 River St. N.
Hermansville, MI 49847
45.70933779841335,
-87.6079552129207

In the small town of Hermansville just off US-2 in the central Upper Peninsula is a large two-story building with a red circle and the letters IXL in the center. The building was built in 1881 by the Wisconsin Land and Lumber Company and used as their office. They made hardwood flooring and branded the flooring IXL for "I excel" to denote the quality of the flooring.

Hermansville was a company town, and the workers lived in housing built by the company. They were paid in script that could be used in the company store. After World War II, the company began selling off its houses into private hands. The company office in Hermansville closed in 1978, and it was converted into a museum in 1982. The museum complex includes a company house, the farm produce warehouse for Wisconsin Land & Lumber, and a restored train depot along with a couple of railroad cars, including a caboose.

Watson

Along County Road 426
46.01961103023635,
-87.4145914135389

If you want to go for a bit of an adventure, County Road 426 cuts across through a more remote section of the Upper Peninsula. It is a rough winding rural road but passes through some small towns. One of the towns is the little town of

Watson near the middle of the Upper Peninsula. Not much of it remains today but a few residents and some old buildings. The town was a sawmill town and mail distribution point with the railroad passing through it. The buildings are privately owned and off limits to people but are next to the road. It reminds me of a ghost town like you would see out west. The buildings are all deteriorated and made of decaying and graying wood. It makes for a nice photo and an interesting place to see. If you like "expanding your horizon", as my dad would say, then 426 is another option besides taking US-2 across the UP.

Crystal Falls

Junction of US-2 and M-69
46.09695463164586,
-88.3339772379724

M-69 and US-2 intersect in the city of Crystal Falls. The Iron County Courthouse stands at the top of the hill overlooking the city. The Richardsonian Romanesque Style building was completed in 1891 and constructed using stone quarried from the nearby Paint River. The town was named for the crystal clear water cascading over the falls on the nearby Paint River. The view from the top of the hill where the courthouse stands is spectacular, and during autumn's peak color, it's breathtaking.

Pictured Rocks Area

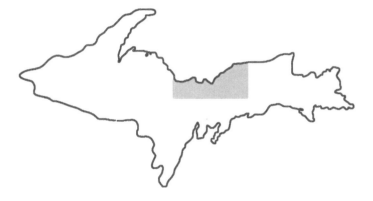

Fox River

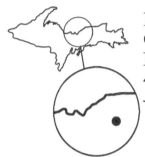

East Branch Fox River
Campground on M-77
Between Seney and Grand Marais
46.468440725140816,
-85.94478980667516

Between Seney and Grand Marais along M-77 is a state forest campground on the east branch of the Fox River. It is not your ordinary campground, and has more than just campsites and outhouses. If you head into the south loop of the campground, you will find a pipe sticking out of the ground that has crystal clear spring water flowing out of it. It is a great place to stop and fill up some water bottles with natural artesian spring water.

Near the spring on the side of a hill is a stone wall and an enormous door. It looks like some sort of medieval cave where a dragon would live. It was built by the Michigan DNR for a fish hatchery that has been gone for several years. Next to the river is a marker for Ernest Hemingway. He came to the area with two of his friends after World War I. He was recovering from injuries after serving as an ambulance driver in the war. He came to the town of Seney with his friends, and they hiked north along the Fox River. The men fished and camped for a week, and young Hemingway fell in love with the area. It was his inspiration for his short story *The Big Two Hearted River*. He never saw the Two Hearted River, but he liked the name better than the Fox River.

The East Branch of the Fox River State River Forest Campground is a nice place to stop for a break and some solitude.

Grand Marais

Lake Ave & Randolph Street
Grand Marais, MI 49839
46.67112305940525,
-85.98468182863503

Along Lake Superior, at the eastern end of Pictured Rocks National Lakeshore, is the town of Grand Marais. In the center of town is a giant brown wooden barrel that stands about twenty feet tall. It is not full of wine nor has it ever held liquid. It was built for cartoonist William Donahey, who created the "Teenie Weenies" syndicated comic strip to use as a summer home.

Donahey was born in Ohio in 1883 and graduated from the Cleveland School of Art. He started his career illustrating children's books. In 1912, he was asked by the Chicago Tribune to develop a comic strip for the newspaper. He created the "Teenie Weenies", a comic strip based on two inch tall characters living among life size objects. The comic strip was syndicated in newspapers around the world. Donahey licensed the little characters for use in advertising and merchandising, making a tidy sum of money from his creation.

Chicago Food Manufacturer Reid Murdock & Co. was just one of the companies that licensed the Teenie Weenies for their advertisements. They hired the Pioneer Cooperage Company of Chicago to design a cabin made of barrels for Dohaney to give to his wife as a gift. The cabin consisted of a large two story barrel with a living room on the first floor and a bedroom on the second floor. A second smaller barrel was attached to the back and used as a kitchen.

The whimsical looking barrel house was erected on the shores of Sable Lake in 1926. The Donaheys used it for a summer home for about ten years. They eventually decided to move the house because so many curious people wanted to see their unique cottage that they were not able to relax as they had planned.

Once it was moved to downtown Grand Marais, the pickle barrel house was used as an ice-cream stand, an information kiosk booth, and a souvenir gift shop. Over the decades, the house fell into disrepair. In 2005, funds were raised by a non profit group, and the historic wooden barrel house was renovated and restored to its original condition. It is now a museum for visitors to see what it looked like when the Donaheys used it as a summer cabin.

Sable Falls

Sable Falls Rd.
Grand Marais, MI 49839
46.66834565857111,
-86.01435920733739

At the eastern end of Pictured Rocks National Lakeshore is Sable Falls. Sable Falls are beautiful secluded waterfalls, cascading down about seventy-five feet, flowing into Lake Superior. A wooden staircase with 169 steps leads down to the falls. Thankfully, there are some resting places along the stairs, if you are like me, and need a break to rest your burning thighs and calves. The beauty of the falls through the dense green forest makes the trip down the stairs worth the effort. At the bottom of the stairs is a viewing platform where you can relax and enjoy watching and listening to the falls. Since it is somewhat out of the way, there are usually few tourists visiting it. The trail continues down to the mouth of the river where it empties into Lake Superior.

Wagner Falls

M-94 south of Munising
46.38885271261335,
-86.64902082517834

The Upper Peninsula is known for its many waterfalls. About a mile outside of Munising, near the intersection of M-28 and M-94, is Wagner Falls. It is an impressive fall with about a twenty foot drop on the Wagner Creek. It is just a short walk down a well-maintained path; at the end is a nice viewing platform for you to just watch and listen as the water cascades down.

Sand Point

N, 8376 Sand Point Rd.
Munising, MI 49862
46.456243192515664,
-86.60728290043177

In 1933, the U.S. Coast Guard built a life-saving station at Sand Point along the Lake Superior shoreline, a few miles northwest of Munising. The building is now used as the headquarters for the Pictured Rocks National Lakeshore. In addition to the main building is an old boat house where the rescue boats were stored. It was also built in 1933. The station was used for decades by the Coast Guard who often aided fishermen whose boats had malfunctioned, towing them back to port. In the winter, they would rescue ice fishermen caught on thin ice.

By 1960, the station had been decommissioned and given to the city of Munising. The city donated it to the National Park Service. The interesting thing about the old boat house is that most of the equipment used by the Coast Guard is still housed in the little building. If you drive past it and the main door is open, be sure to stop and visit. You can see the historic artifacts along with a couple of boats that are on display with signage explaining what they were used for.

Christmas Lighthouse

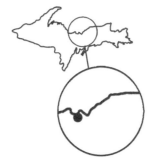

E10102 M-28,
Munising, MI 49862
46.43735830655035,
-86.69138549371928

West of Munising along Lake Superior and M-28 is the town of Christmas. Gamblers know of the town for the large "log cabin" style casino that welcomes people wanting to try their luck. Tourists to the Upper Peninsula know about the little town because of its unique name. The town got its name in 1938, when Julius Thorton built a factory to make holiday gifts. I am confused as to whether he named the town or his factory Christmas. Unfortunately, in the summer of 1940, the business burned down and was never rebuilt. The workshop no longer exists, but the area kept the name Christmas.

After the Civil War, as shipping increased on Lake Superior, many vessels sailed between Grand Island and the mainland to seek refuge from the numerous storms. A pair of lights, known as range lights, were erected on the shoreline near Christmas to guide sailors into the channel. A small wooden tower was built near the edge of Lake Superior and a lighthouse was constructed further back.

By the early 1900s, the Grand Island Harbor Range lighthouse was in need of repair, so the decision was made to replace it and the keeper with an automated system. A conical iron tower was constructed in 1913, with an acetylene light that would automatically ignite when the sun valve opened. When the sun went down, the valve would automatically open and the gas eliminated the need for electricity to be run to the lighthouse.

By the 1960s, ships were so large that many could not use the narrow passage around Grand Island for safety. In 1969, the rear light was decommissioned and permanently turned off. It is not an overly impressive lighthouse, but it is one of the tallest iron tower navigational lights on the Great Lakes. It is currently under the ownership and care of the National Forest Service and is part of the Hiawatha National Forest.

If you want to visit the old iron tower, the easiest way to find it is to look for the "Welcome to Christmas" sign east of town. There is a sandy parking area and a trail that leads to the water and front range light. A two track road leads to the old iron tower across the road.

Bay Furnace

Bay Furnace Rd.
Munising, MI 49862
46.44210469862648,
-86.70551114898359

Bay Furnace Campground sits west of Christmas off M-28. Here you will find the ruins of an old iron smelting furnace that gives the campground its name. There is a parking area along the driveway to the campground that has a short trail that leads to the ruins. They were built in the 1870s and were part of the town of Onota. The town burned down in 1877, and all that remains is the stone furnace. Not only is it an interesting historic site to check out, but it has a great view of Lake Superior.

Marquette Area

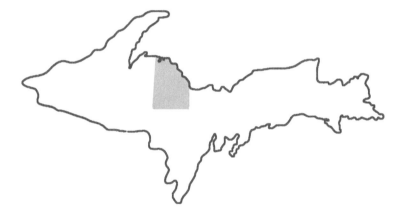

Marquette

Marquette Harbor Lighthouse
300 N. Lakeshore Blvd.
Marquette, MI 49855
46.54705141649633,
-87.37620418786624

Marquette is the largest city in the Upper Peninsula and home to Northern Michigan University. The downtown area has several historic buildings which house many locally owned shops and restaurants. Not far from downtown along the Lake Superior shoreline is a massive structure. It was the lower harbor ore dock used to load iron ore into freighters. It closed in the 1970s, but the ore dock north of town near Presque Isle Park is still in use, and often in the summer, you will see ships being loaded. Presque Isle Park is a popular spot in the summertime where swimmers can jump off the Black Rocks into Lake Superior.

Standing on a rocky shoreline is a large two story red lighthouse that guides ships into Marquette Harbor. It is one of the oldest structures in the Upper Peninsula's largest city. It was constructed in 1865 to replace an earlier lighthouse that was constructed in the 1850s. It was one of the first lighthouses built on Lake Superior. The area around Marquette was rich with iron ore deposits which is how it became a prominent city in the UP.

When the current lighthouse was constructed, it was only one and a half stories tall. In 1910, an assistant keeper was needed to help with the fog signal and breakwater light. A second story was added as living quarters for the assistant keeper. In 1965, the lighthouse was painted red to make it more visible in the daytime. The Coast Guard operated the lighthouse as a residence for some of the coasties stationed in Marquette, but the last resident moved out in 1998.

The lighthouse is now owned by the city of Marquette. The nearby Maritime Museum gives tours of the historic lighthouse. On occasion, tour guides and visitors have seen the ghost of a little girl wearing a 1910s style dress. Sometimes she is seen staring out of the window over Lake Superior or on the catwalk around the lantern. She seems to like showing her spirit to women and other children.

There was no reported death of a little girl at the lighthouse. However, near the turn of the century, a keeper's young daughter was badly injured when she fell on the rocks at the shoreline. I don't know if it is actually haunted, but strangely, a lot of keepers have abruptly resigned their duties while serving at the big red lighthouse.

Negaunee

Jackson Mine Park
199 Tobin St.
Negaunee, MI 49866
46.498692719375455,
-87.62181129559153

In the area southwest of Negaunee, you will find several old staircases built in the berms and hills that lead to nowhere. This region of the city is known as Old Town and had several houses and buildings surrounding the Jackson Mine. The mine was the first iron ore mine in the Lake Superior region. In 1844, surveyor William Burt noticed some strange fluctuations on his compass and upon further investigation, he noticed iron ore deposits. Soon afterwards, the first mine was dug. The mine closed in the 1950s and is now a historic site.

Several structures in the area have collapsed due to shafts underneath caving in. Because of the unstable grounds, the buildings in Old Town have been either moved or demolished. It is now part of a park that the Heritage Trail passes through. You can still drive down the old streets and see several staircases that once led to homes in Old Town. In 2003, the area was converted into a park by the city of Negaunee and has mining artifacts on display.

Big Bay

Big Bay Lighthouse B&B
4674 Co Rd KCB
Big Bay, MI 49808
46.843169982387394,
-87.68038805825354

Standing on a tall rocky bluff overlooking Lake Superior is the Big Bay Point Lighthouse built in 1897 near the town of Big Bay. The house was built as a duplex with one side for the head lighthouse keeper and the other for the assistant keeper. Those who worked at Big Bay Point were truly isolated. The keepers' wives not only had to do the usual housekeeping and food preparation, but also schooling of any children in residence.

The first keeper William Prior made the twenty-four-mile walk to Marquette to visit his dying sister. After her funeral, he walked back to the lighthouse and discovered that the assistant keeper was not fulfilling his duties. After firing him and a couple more incompetent assistant keepers, Prior hired his son George to be the assistant keeper. Just over a year after George was hired, he fell on the steps of the landing crib. Keeper Prior took him to the hospital in Marquette on April 18, 1901, and his son passed away roughly two months later on June 13. His son's death drove him into a deep depression, and on June 28, he disappeared into the woods with his gun and some strychnine. It was feared that he had gone off to kill himself. A search party was sent out, but they were not able to find him.

Over a year later, the following entry was made in the station log:

Mr. Fred Babcock came to the station 12:30 pm. While hunting in the woods one and a half mile south of the station this noon he found a skeleton of a man hanging to a tree. We went to the place with him and found that the clothing and everything tally with the former keeper of this station who has been missing for seventeen months.

By 1941, the light was automated, and in 1951-1952, the building and land were leased to the U.S. Army. Soldiers were stationed at the lighthouse for two-week periods of anti-aircraft artillery training. Large guns were placed on the cliff near the lighthouse, and targets were towed by planes over Lake Superior for practice. The soldiers lived in the meadow and woods to the west of the lighthouse. One of the soldiers stationed at the lighthouse murdered the owner of the Lumberjack Tavern, in the town of Big Bay, for raping his wife. The book and movie *Anatomy Of A Murder* are based on the crime.

1961, the Lighthouse and surrounding property were sold to a private owner. Today it is the only operational lighthouse with a bed and breakfast. Rumor has it that the lighthouse is still haunted by the ghost of Keeper Prior. I am not sure it is, but I do know it is a beautiful lighthouse, and would be a nice place to stay at.

Alder Falls

Alder Creek Truck Trail
Off County Rd. 550
46.78293130249311,
-87.70519245382997

Located northwest of Marquette, Alder Falls can be a little tricky to find as it is on a two-track road, off County Road 550, near Big Bay. After parking near a little wooden sign for the falls, you need to hike down into a gorge to see the waterfalls. There are no steps, so it can be difficult to climb down and back up, especially for someone out of shape like me. I think that is why I like these falls so much; they are hard to access and find, so usually there is not a large crowd of people. The times that I visited the falls, no one else was around, and it was a peaceful place to relax and enjoy the waterfalls as the water rushed around the large rocks in the river

510 Bridge

510 County Rd. Where it crosses over the Dead River Negaunee, MI 49866 46.55844487749207, -87.54619339107606

Big Bay Road will take travelers along the Lake Superior shoreline to Big Bay from Marquette. County Road 510 is another road to Big Bay, and it connects with US-41 about ten miles west of Marquette. A bridge crosses over the Dead River along 510. From the new bridge, you can get an incredible view of the old steel truss bridge below. There is a parking lot on the southeast side of the new bridge for travelers to stop and admire the view. You can also drive down to the old bridge. Cars are no longer permitted to drive across the old bridge, but you can walk across it.

Huron Mountains Area

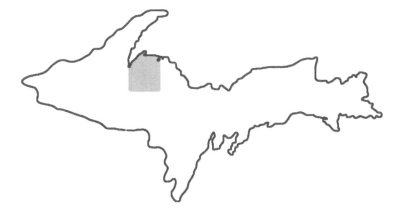

Michigamme

Michigamme Museum
110 W Main St.
Michigamme, MI 49861
46.535653732087766,
-88.1090173680114

The town of Michigamme is west of Marquette and sits between US-41/M-28 and Lake Michigamme. It was founded around a mine discovered by Jacob Houghton. Mining operations ended in the early 1900s, and the population of the town dwindled. It is more of a resort town now, being situated on the shores of Lake Michigamme. It is an interesting place with shops, restaurants, and a lot of history. The Michigamme Museum stands near the center of town and holds several artifacts from the region, including an early 1900s horse drawn fire fighting pumper.

Next to the museum is an old log cabin house with two doors. The original builder of the house was the Michigamme Mining Company and was one of the first structures in town. It has two entry doors because it was most likely a duplex when it was built. In 1896, Napoleon Beauvais purchased the home from the mining company. He and his wife, Julia Cadair Beauvias, moved in. Unfortunately, in 1903, Beauvais' son from his first marriage attacked Julia and then killed himself. Julia was able to summon help before she died herself. The home remained vacant until 1916 when Eusebe Dompierre purchased the home for his daughter and her family for $200, which would be about $4560 today. The home remained in the Dompierre family until it was moved to its present location and restored in 2000.

The first Moose Lift took place in Michigamme in 1985. During a ten-day period, nineteen cows and ten bull moose were captured in Canada, and released just north of

Michigamme. In 1987, a second moose lift relocated another thirty moose. The historic town is easy to miss when you are traveling along US-41 since it passes next to it instead of through it. But it is a nice town to stop and explore.

Rock Cut

Off the Huron Bay Peshekee Grade Road in the Huron Mountains
46.73349840761702,
-88.17468702215088

Deep in the forests of the Huron Mountains is a huge gash in the solid rock terrain. It was created in the 1890s to run the Iron Range and Huron Bay Railroad from Champion to an ore dock near Skanee. A group of investors in the Detroit area thought they could make a fortune on hauling iron ore by train from a mine near Champion. They spent about two million dollars and employed 1500 men building a railroad and ore dock. By the time it was completed, the mine had stopped producing iron ore and the railroad was no longer needed. Shortly after, the railroad was sold for about $100,000, and the tracks were removed and used downstate.

The Huron Bay Peshekee Grade Road from US-41 will take you near the famed rock cut. The road follows along the Peshekee River and was constructed using part of the old railroad grade. It is not a trip for the faint of heart. It is about twenty miles of rough road back into the wilderness. It takes about forty-five minutes to drive one way to the cut. Although it was a long and rough trip back to the rock cut, it was one of the most impressive things I have seen in Michigan. I can only imagine what kind of hell the men endured to create it, only for it to never be utilized.

Canyon Falls

Roadside park a few miles
south of Alberta
Old US Hwy 41,
L'Anse, MI 49946
46.628891772736985,
-88.47055200703201

Canyon Falls is about fifteen miles south of L'Anse. The trail to the falls begins at a roadside park on US-41, and it is one of the most popular tourist destinations in the area. Known for its scenic beauty, the waterfall is about 30 feet high and is located in a box canyon. The canyon walls are made of unique square rock that makes for sharp ledges and man-made-looking walls. The trail leading to the falls is about one mile long, and is suitable for people of all ages and abilities. The hike is not difficult, but it can be slow as the trail gets muddy and has a lot of tree roots to step over. Unlike some roadside park waterfalls that are near the park, plan on taking a couple of hours to see these magnificent falls. The canyon is open year-round, but the best time to visit is during the spring or fall when the water levels are high.

Alberta Sawmill

21235 Alberta Ave # 2,
L'Anse, MI 49946
46.64455000599862,
-88.48098876289842

A few miles south of L'Anse on U.S. 41 is Alberta, where Henry Ford built a sawmill town in 1936 to supply lumber to his growing auto company. The town was named after the daughter of one of his executives. The community consisted of a sawmill, houses for the workers and their families, and two schools to educate the children while their parents were working. In 1954, the town of Alberta was donated to Michigan Tech and is still used today for forestry education. They give tours of the historic town and sawmill to visitors.

Pequaming

16542 Hebard Ave,
L'Anse, MI 49946
46.85118350466842,
-88.40293786580018

North of L'Anse on the Keweenaw Bay is a point that creates a natural harbor. The Ojibwe Indians had a settlement on the point called Pequaming. In the Ojibwe language, Pequaming means "headlands". In 1877, Charles Hebard and Edward Thurber purchased large tracts of land in the area and built a sawmill in Pequaming. Shortly after the company was formed, Thurber sold his half to Hebard. With the help of his sons, Charles Hebard's company became one of the largest sawmills in the Upper Peninsula. At its peak, they employed about a thousand workers and produced thirty million board feet of lumber per year.

After Charles Heberd died in 1904, his sons inherited the company. They had great success in the lumbering business and in 1913 built a summer home in Pequaming known as "the bungalow". Ford Motor Company approached the brothers in 1922 about purchasing land for timber to produce wood parts for the Model T. The brothers convinced Henry Ford to purchase their whole operation for 2.8 million dollars. Ford purchased the sawmill and most of the buildings in the town, and used the bungalow as his summer home.

Pequaming became a company town, and Ford used it as a model community for his beliefs on self reliance and education. He built new schools for the workers' children, and his summer home was used for vocational training during the winter. With increased shipping costs, and the fact that wood was used less in the manufacturing of automobiles, Ford shut down the mill in 1942. The town slowly declined over the years, and most of the mill is gone. The brick powerhouse building remains along with the water tower that still has the Ford logo painted on it. The bungalow also stands along the bay and is privately owned but can be rented for various occasions. The buildings are privately owned, so please do not go poking around them, but you can drive through the town and see them from your vehicle.

Mt Arvon

In the Middle of the Huron Mountains
46.75785852543476, -88.15571489451013

The highest natural point in Michigan is the summit of Mount Arvon in the Huron Mountain Range, which lies between Marquette and L'Anse. Mt. Arvon's peak is 1979 feet above sea level, and a sign marks the highest point at the top. It has a U.S. Geological Survey benchmark (round metal marker) and a mailbox with a logbook for visitors to sign and record that they stood on Great Lakes State's highest point.

If you are physically fit and adventurous, you might want to walk around the two-mile hiking trail that leads to the summit. If the thought of hiking two miles uphill sounds like torture, you can drive right up to it. Mt. Arvon is about a thirty-mile trek from L'Anse. The last fifteen miles are up winding gravel forest roads that make the destination a real accomplishment to visit. You could probably drive to it in a passenger car, but I would recommend an SUV or truck. It would be best to make the journey in the summer months, avoiding early spring when there is still snow on the roads in the Huron Mountains. The snow also makes the roads muddy and impassable at times. If you take the trip, be sure to stop at the Baraga Convention and Visitors Bureau in L'Anse for directions and info on road conditions.

If you are looking for a place in Michigan to add to your bucket list, this is a good one. Just be sure to plan on a couple of hours driving there and back from L'Anse. One last thing—do not rely on your GPS to take you there. You want to get to Mt. Arvon by driving south on Roland Lake Road from Skanee Road. Follow the light blue diamond signs that direct motorists to the summit.

Herman

Intersection of
Herman and Lystila Roads
46.66645350891612,
-88.36706420166794

The town of Herman is located in a remote section of the Huron Mountains southeast of L'Anse. The town was named for lumberjack Herman Keranen who took up farming in the area. Over the decades the population has dwindled and it is mostly a ghost town. There are a few empty buildings still standing. An old store sits along the railroad tracks, and what looks like an old boarding house is on the other side of the road. It is in rough shape with the roof collapsed from all the snow. On December 19, 1996, the town received one of the largest snowfalls in Michigan history, with 30 inches of the white stuff falling in the single day. There are a few houses and an old Co-op hall still standing in town. Nestria Herman Road passes through the woods and the town of Herman at an angle kind of like a "short cut", but it is definitely not faster than taking US-41 because it is a winding dirt road. It is a scenic trip, but I recommend doing it in a four wheel drive truck or SUV.

Powerhouse Falls

Power House Road
L'Anse, 49946
46.737098391067924,
-88.44431692174724

A few miles south of L'Anse is Powerhouse Falls, aptly named for the old abandoned powerhouse that is next to the falls. The waterfall is the largest one on the Falls River. It is a beautiful waterfall that is easy to access and has a nice picnic area to take a break on a long journey. I also find it one of the more interesting waterfalls in Michigan with the juxtaposition of majestic natural waterfalls next to the old abandoned man-made power house, the old building that makes these falls unique. I think that is what makes the Upper Peninsula such a spectacular place to visit. It is the combination of natural wonders and historic sites that make exploring it so much fun. The falls are easy to find, and they are not far from US-41. If you turn west onto Dam Road and go down it about a mile, it winds around to a parking lot for the falls.

Keweenaw Area

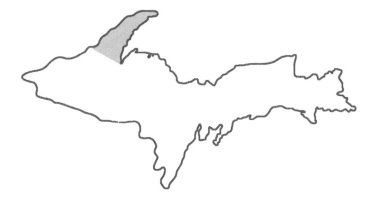

Assinins

Intersection of Assinins Rd. and Old US Hwy 41
46.81087077449111,
-88.47731007338524

North of Baraga is what remains of the town of Assinins, one of the earliest settlements in the region. Bishop Frederic Baraga frequently did missionary work with the local Native Americans in the Upper Peninsula. He was invited to visit the area along the Keweenaw Bay by Chief Edward Assinins. In

1843, Bishop Baraga established a Catholic Mission, and for decades it was simply known as the Catholic Mission. Baraga lived in the mission for a short time, and it was there that he wrote an Ojibwe dictionary that was published in 1853. The dictionary remains an important tool for translating the Ojibwe and Chippewa language into English to this day. In 1894, the mission was given a post office and officially named Assinins after the Indian Chief.

The village started with several log cabins and a church. In 1860, Baraga built the St. Joseph Orphanage and School. The original building was destroyed by fire, and a new larger stone building was built to replace it, along with a rectory and convent. In 1929, another large three story orphanage was built, and at its peak, it had 950 orphans, both Native American and white children. The structures were last used in the 1960s and in recent years have collapsed. Only a small portion of the orphanage is still standing, hidden behind the trees. The area is now part of the Keweenaw Bay Indian Community and is listed as a National Historic District.

Hanka Homestead

13249 Hanka
Baraga, MI 49908
46.896704757624995,
-88.53893028449562

In the forest near the base of the Keweenaw Peninsula, is the old Hanka Homestead. The historic farm is one of only a few historical farms that has its original buildings in their original locations. Visiting this secluded early 20th century farm is like stepping back in time.

Herman Hanka was born in Finland in 1848. After emigrating to America, he was injured in a mine explosion near Calumet in 1888. In 1896, his daughter applied for and received the eighty acres that became the Hanka farm. The family logged some of the timber to build a house and over the years constructed several more buildings, including a barn, grist mill, blacksmith shop and sauna. The family lived off the land, growing vegetables in the summer, and hunting rabbits and deer for meat throughout the year.

Herman died in 1933, and his wife Wilhelmina died in 1942 at the age of 93. Their son, and youngest child, Jallu died in 1966; he was the last Hanka to live on the old homestead. The old farm sat vacant for about fifteen years before it was restored to its 1920s condition. The grounds are open all year, and the buildings are open to visitors in the summer time for a small donation.

Freda Ruins

Superior View Rd.
Atlantic Mine, 49905
47.135524667041075,
-88.82220332506789

Along the shoreline of Lake Superior are a tall smokestack and concrete ruins. They are near the town of Freda west of Houghton in the Keweenaw Peninsula. The maze of weathered concrete and rusty rebar are what remain of the

Champion Mill that processed the copper-rich rocks. Trains would pull into the mill and dump their cars filled with copper-infused rocks. The mill would pulverize the rocks and mix them with water from Lake Superior, creating a sludge rich in copper. It was taken by train to Houghton for further processing and then poured into ingots and shipped around the world. The mill closed in 1967, and it was stripped of any metal for scrap. A small park with a veterans memorial at the end of Superior View Road overlooks the ruins.

Redridge Dam

Where S-554 (Liminga Rd.)
crosses the Salmon Trout River
47.14910010385337,
-88.76428357608728

When I first saw it, I was not sure if this was a bridge, a dam, or a waterfall. This massive steel structure spans the Salmon Trout River near the town of Redridge. Water flows underneath and through its rusty girders, and it looks as if it has been standing for a long time.

It is one of only three steel dams built in the United States. It was constructed across the Salmon Trout River in 1901 for the Atlantic Mining Company. The mine operated for about twenty years and then went out of business, making the reservoir unnecessary. Over time, the dam deteriorated, and holes were cut into the steel in 1979 to lower the water level and allow the current to flow over the remains of the steel dam. When I visited, there were a few Yoopers fishing along the shoreline. I assume the fishing is good, and maybe that is how the Salmon Trout River got its name. A small parking lot on Road S-554 near the dam has a trail that leads to the base of the dam. Another trail leads to an older wooden dam that preceded the steel one.

The Stone Ship

Kearsarge Veterans Memorial
US-41 and Smith Ave.
Calumet, MI 49913
47.26936897777653,
-88.42027502786061

North of Calumet, US-41 winds through the center of the Keweenaw Peninsula. The road passes by Veterans Memorial Park in the town of Kearsarge. At the center of the park is a large stone ship with a mining drill mounted on the bow, representing a gun.

The town was named for the Civil War ship *U.S.S. Kearsarge* by one of the ship's officers who moved to the Keweenaw after the war. By the 1930s, the Great Depression had severely cut copper production and mining in the Upper Peninsula, and workers were in desperate need of support. Franklin D. Roosevelt's New Deal provided government-sponsored work programs to give people jobs on civilian projects. The WPA (Works Progress Administration) built many of the area's bridges, public buildings, and roads. In 1934, the WPA built the stone ship that sits along the road in Kearsarge. It does not resemble the Civil War ship or any of the other four U.S. Navy ships that were named *Kearsarge*, but the forty-foot-long stone ship is a nice tribute to these ships and the men and women who served on them.

The WPA built three ships. One was near Hancock and has crumbled into a pile of rocks. The other still stands north of Calumet near the corner of 1st and Jefferson Streets.

Central Mine

Central Rd. and Old Stage Rd.
Near Mohawk
47.407537462537455,
-88.20087420875252

US-41 is the main road through the center of the Keweenaw Peninsula. Travelers may notice a little sign for the Central Mine Visitors Center between Calumet and Copper Harbor. Many tourists pass by without even thinking of stopping. I think few people realize there is a whole ghost town to explore that is open to the public.

In 1854, John Shawson, a local miner, discovered copper in the region and the Central Mining Company was formed. A company town was built around the mining operation and given the same name as the company. The town's population grew to over nine hundred people. More than one hundred structures were built, which included houses, mining buildings and a church. Many of the miners were immigrants from Cornwall, England, bringing with them their meat-filled pastry recipes; these pastries are popular in the Upper Peninsula. By the late 1890s, the copper had been depleted, and Central Mine turned off the pumps and sealed the shafts. By 1950, the last permanent residents had left the once prosperous town.

The Keweenaw County Historical Society owns thirty-eight acres of the old Central Mine site and town. It operates the Visitors Center, which is located in a former house. The society has also restored several other houses and buildings in the old town. Some are open to visitors and decorated with antiques from the period they were built. When I visited, the small town was strangely quiet. I could walk through the open houses and explore the area. It was like stepping back in time. Visitors can walk into a house over a century old and see items on display that date back to the mining days.

Eagle Harbor

670 Lighthouse Rd.
Eagle Harbor, MI 49950
47.459834767463526,
-88.15915997416417

Many of the lighthouses that stand in Michigan on the Great Lakes are on a sandy shoreline. The Eagle Harbor Lighthouse, however, sits atop a rocky harbor entrance, making for a picturesque scene popular with photographers and artists. Since the mid 1800s, ships have sailed into Eagle Harbor in the Keweenaw Peninsula to seek refuge from Lake Superior storms. The first lighthouse, built in the 1850s, was a stone house with a wooden tower. It was evident that this was inadequate, and in the 1870s, the current red brick lighthouse was built. Ships' captains had difficulty spotting the lighthouse in the daytime, with the red brick blending into the surrounding natural rocks, so part of the lighthouse was painted white. Other houses and buildings were added to the lighthouse grounds for the assistant keepers and members of the U.S. Lifesaving Service. In 1962, the lighthouse was converted to an electric light. Because the lighthouse was automated, it was determined that no one needed to be stationed at Eagle Harbor. The last person to live at the lighthouse was transferred to a different duty in 1982.

Some say the old lighthouse is haunted. It is believed to be the ghost of Stephen Cocking. After serving in the Civil War in the 23rd Michigan Volunteer Infantry Regiment, he moved back to the Upper Peninsula. He became the lighthouse keeper in 1877 and tended the light until he died at the lighthouse of pneumonia in 1889.

The Coast Guard still operates and maintains the light in the tower, but the lighthouse is owned by the Keweenaw County Historical Society. It is open for tours from June to October. Across the harbor from the lighthouse is the Eagle Harbor Marina. It has a few buildings that were used by the Lifesaving Service and a great view of the lighthouse. It also has a beautiful park-like area that is a wonderful place for a picnic.

Cliff Mine

Cliff Drive north of Ahmeek
47.37327461230359,
-88.31301499510475

North of Calumet deep in the forests at the center of the Keweenaw Peninsula are the stone ruins of a once prosperous mine and the town that supported it. Legend has it that copper was discovered in 1845 when a prospector was exploring the area and fell off the cliff. He injured his derriere, or as Forrest Gump would say "buttocks", on a piece of protruding copper.

The Cliff Mine was the first successful mine in the Michigan Copper District. The highly successful mine was the largest copper mine in the US for more than a decade after it was started. By the 1870s, the veins of copper had been extracted from the ground and the mine closed.

You can still see the stone walls and foundations from the buildings among the trees behind the tailings (piles of rocks) dug out from the mine. You can find the old Cliff Mine ruins at a spot east of Cliff Road. A wooden sign marks the spot where the ruins can be seen in the woods on the other side of the west branch of the Eagle River. When I visited, a makeshift bridge out of lumber crossed a narrow spot in the river. Be sure to walk up and down the river for a spot to cross. The location is also a favorite with rock hounds to look for stones.

North of the little town of Mohawk on US-41 is a sign for the Cliff Cemetery. The sign seems out of place because you cannot see a cemetery. The cemetery does exist but it is hidden in the woods. After hiking about fifty yards into the forest, you will see tombstones standing quietly among the trees. The ground is covered by green leafy plants, which I think is wintergreen. Paths snake through the thick growth to the various grave sites. In the back of the cemetery is an old stone foundation left over from the chapel that once stood next to the tombstones.

Quincy Dredge

On the shoreline of Torch Lake
Seen from M-26 about ten
miles north of Hancock
47.14927980317246,
-88.46139119178133

If you are traveling through the Keweenaw Peninsula on M-26, you will come across this giant metal monster, rusting away on the shoreline of Torch Lake (This is a different Torch Lake than the one near Traverse City). After copper was discovered in the Keweenaw Peninsula, many mining operations began to extract the valuable metal from the ore mined in the region. Stamping mills were built to crush the ore and separate the copper. The ore that was pounded down to sand was washed out into a nearby lake or river.

The Quincy Mining Company Stamp Mill built in 1888 near Torch Lake was one of several stamp mills in the area, and as the mills became more efficient, the sand in the lake was reclaimed and reprocessed to extract the copper that was missed in earlier processing. The Calumet and Hecla Mining Company had the dredge built in 1914 to retrieve the sand from Torch Lake for their mill in the city of Lake Linden. In 1951, the Quincy Mining Company purchased the dredge and named it Quincy Dredge Number Two since they already owned another dredge. During the winter layup in 1967, the dredge sank and with the company struggling to make a profit, they just left it where it sank, and it still sits there to this day.

In 1978, the state declared it an historic site. Across from the dredge near M-26 are The Quincy Mining Company Stamp Mills Historic District, with the remains of Stamp Mill Number One.

Brockway Mountain

Brockway Mountain Dr.
47.46455071513148,
-87.96902165923572

Brockway Mountain is located between Copper Harbor and Eagle Harbor. At its highest point, it is over 1300 feet above sea level and has a breathtaking view of Lake Superior and the Keweenaw Wilderness. There is a parking area and a lookout at the peak along with a few other lookouts on the eight-mile-long Brockway Mountain Drive scenic route. At the western end, a lookout overlooks the town of Copper Harbor and gives tourists a bird's eye view of the historic town. The road is paved but winding and rough across the mountain. If you drive this road, take your time because there is usually a lot of traffic from sightseers. I have also seen people pulling large travel trailers on the road, but I don't recommend it, and you should avoid pulling a trailer if you can.

Calumet

Italian Hall Memorial
423 7th St.
Calumet, MI 49913
47.248415472814216,
-88.45520979965083

Red Jacket Fire Station
327 6th St,
Calumet, MI 49913
47.247400516313995,
-88.4540391649493

Near the corner of 7th and Elm Streets in Calumet is an old stone archway standing in a small park. It is a reminder of a tragic day in the history of Copper Country. The town of Calumet was one of the wealthiest towns in the United States in the late 1800s because of its copper deposits and mining industry. On Christmas Eve in 1913, after being on strike for five months, copper miners and their families gathered for a yuletide party on the second floor of the Italian Hall in Calumet. During the party for the striking miners, someone yelled, "Fire!" Although there was no fire, seventy-three people died while attempting to escape down a stairwell.

Over half of those who died were children between the ages of six and ten. The narrow stairway became congested by people fleeing for the exit, and after the first person fell, it became a "domino effect" with people being trampled. The tragic event was part of the reason building codes were enacted for building capacity and fire escapes. The Italian Hall was built in 1908, and the two-story red brick building was razed in 1984, but the doorway with its stone arch was left standing as a memorial to the people who lost their lives in the 1913 disaster.

A block away on the corner of 6th and Elm is the historic Calumet Theatre. The theater opened on March 20, 1900. It had an electric chandelier made from copper to illuminate its ornately decorated interior. Some of the most popular and talented actors performed on its stage, including Douglas Fairbanks, Lon Chaney Sr. and the world-renowned Polish actress Helena Modjeska. Even the great Harry Houdini performed his magical escapes on its stage. The popularity of motion pictures replaced live performances in the 1920s. The old theater is said to be haunted by the ghosts of some of the actors who graced its stage. It was also used as a temporary morgue after the Italian Hall disaster.

Across the street from the old theater is the Red Jacket Fire Department. The city of Calumet in the Keweenaw Peninsula was settled in 1864, originally under the name of "Red Jacket", named for a Native American Chief of the Seneca tribe. The Calumet and Hecla Mine was the dominant company in the town, and in 1929 the town's name was officially changed to Calumet.

The city has several large stone Richardson Romanesque style buildings constructed with red sandstone that were built at a time when copper was king and the city had money. Since the mines closed, it is as if the town was stuck in time, and the old buildings still remain. The Keweenaw National Historical Park Calumet Visitor Center welcomes tourists to show the area's history. Downtown you will find shops and restaurants if you are looking for souvenirs or to get a bite to eat.

Houghton - Hancock

US- 41 in the heart of the
Keweenaw
47.1237067725149,
-88.57399578186678

Houghton is full of wonderful shops and restaurants as well as a beautiful waterfront park overlooking the Keweenaw waterway and the lift bridge, which crosses over it. On the other side of the water is the town of Hancock, and you can see the historic remains of the Quincy Smelting Works. The area is full of natural beauty and man-made historic landmarks. The cities of Houghton and Hancock are connected by the Portage Lake Lift Bridge (officially, the Houghton–Hancock Bridge). US Highway 41 and M-26 are both routed across the bridge.

The bridge is the world's heaviest and widest double-decked vertical-lift bridge, and its center span "lifts" to provide 100 feet of clearance for ships. The bottom deck originally had railroad tracks for trains to cross the bridge. Rail traffic ended in the 1980s. The bridge is raised to allow cars to pass over the lower deck and boats can sail under the bridge. During the winter months, the bridge is lowered so that cars can use the upper deck and snowmobiles can use the lower deck.

Haven Falls

6280 Gay Lac La Belle Rd.
Mohawk, MI 49950
47.38221014198944,
-88.02877900934213

Haven Falls sits at the western end of Lac La Belle Lake. It is not the tallest or largest waterfall in the Keweenaw, but it is a spectacular waterfall in a wonderful roadside park. The creek flows through the center of the park, and picnic tables are situated around the park for an excellent place to eat while watching the water cascade down.

Gay

925 Lake St,
Lake Linden, MI 49945
47.227531620270554,
-88.16297954905745

Lac Labelle Road travels along the eastern side of the Keweenaw for spectacular views of the bay. It also passes through the town of Gay. Mostly known for the Gay Bar, the town has an old school building converted into a museum. Just south of town, you will see a large smokestack towering above the trees. It was part of the old Mohawk and Wolverine Stamp Mill. Rail cars full of ore would come into the mill and dump the ore, where it would be pulverized and the copper extracted. The remaining sand would be conveyed out to the Lake Superior shoreline. The mill operated from 1900 to 1932 and produced 22 million metric tons of sand. A trail leads to the base of the chimney, and from there you can see the foundations of the old mill.

Clark Mine

Clark Mine Rd. South of
Copper Harbor
47.445292976797,
-87.86054863615291

This old chimney stands in the woods east of Copper Harbor and Lake Fanny Hooe. The old smokestack is all that remains of the Clark Mine. It was first dug in 1853 and operated by a few different companies until it closed in 1901. All that remains is this old chimney and an area covered in rocks and stone. It is a popular spot for rock hunters and not too difficult to find. Taking Manganese Road next to the Copper Harbor Visitors Center east, it will curve into Clark Mine Rd. About a mile down the road, you will see a wooden sign for the old mine.

Rocket Range

Rocket Range Trail,
Copper Harbor, MI 49918
47.43245674538114,
-87.71397217672808

The northernmost point of the Michigan mainland is the tip of the Keweenaw Peninsula. It was from this remote location that NASA and the University of Michigan launched rockets. The project was led by WWII pilot Dr. Harold Allen, who was a Professor of Aeronautics at the University of Michigan. Starting in 1964, the team launched about fifty "Mighty Mouse" rockets from floating buoys between the shoreline and Manitou Island. The rockets were part of the WEBOC project, which was a proposed system of ocean buoys that would launch rockets in the atmosphere to relay weather information. Later in the 60s, larger Arca rockets, which stood six feet tall, were launched from the site. The site was started by pouring a concrete slab and having a rocket launcher trucked to the remote location from White Sands, New Mexico. Launches were done in the winter months when logging and shipping were finished for the season.

In December 1971, a 1700-pound Nike Apache two stage rocket standing 28 feet tall was launched from the site. That was the last rocket to be sent into the sky from the Keweenaw Peninsula. All the buildings and equipment were removed. All that remains at the site is the concrete slab with an iron rail. A stone marker was placed on the concrete launching pad in 2000, marking the historic location.

The launch site is open to the public and offers a spectacular view of Lake Superior from the rugged shoreline. Getting to the site can be a challenge. At the end of US-41 is a rough dirt road. After traveling the dirt road for several miles, you come to a narrow trail requiring a four wheel drive vehicle to drive down it. I definitely would not attempt it in the spring. In the winter, you can reach the site by snowmobile.

Fort Wilkins

15223 US Hwy 41.
Copper Harbor, MI 49918
47.467823125947845,
-87.86210405983245

Two centuries ago, Copper Harbor was isolated and nearly inaccessible, but that did not prevent the copper boom. The abundance of copper in the region and the natural harbor gave the town its name. As the population of miners grew, the U.S. government decided that it was necessary to build a military fort to protect the copper mines from the British and to keep the peace with the local Native Americans.

Fort Wilkins was established along the shoreline of Lake Fanny Hooe in 1844 and was named for the Secretary of War William Wilkins. Twenty-seven structures were built, including a guardhouse, powder magazine, officer's quarters, two barracks, two mess halls, a hospital, a bakery, and a blacksmith's shop. After two years, the fort was deemed unnecessary and the men stationed at it were sent to Texas to fight in the war with Mexico. Sergeant William Wright stayed as a single caretaker of the fort until his death in 1855.

The fort was briefly used after the Civil War because the U.S. Army needed a place for men to serve out the rest of their enlistments. I have a feeling they were not happy about being sent to the tip of the Keweenaw. It must have felt more like a punishment, especially in winter. By 1870, the fort had been completely abandoned by the military. In 1923, the fort and nearby lighthouse became a state park. In 1939, with help from the Work Projects Administration (WPA), the few remaining original buildings were renovated and the rest of the fort was reconstructed. A campground and shower buildings were also created at that time.

Today, Fort Wilkins Historic State Park serves as both a campground and a historic site, welcoming visitors throughout the summer. It is a wonderful place to roam around, exploring the buildings to see and feel what it must have been like to live in the remote fort in the mid 1800s.

Western UP

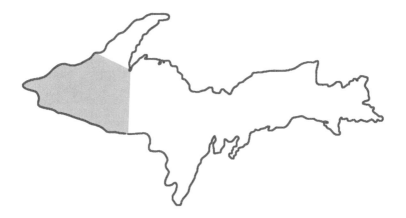

Porcupine Mountains

Porcupine Mts. Vistors Center
33303 Headquarters Rd.
Ontonagon, MI 49953
46.81661792819565,
-89.62513175669908

Porcupine Mountains Wilderness State Park has over sixty thousand acres and is the largest state park in Michigan. It can take thirty minutes to drive from Lake of the Clouds in the east end of the park to the Presque Isle River in the west. You can easily spend a day in the park visiting the many scenic sites and hiking the trails. At the east end of the park is the Visitors

Center with information and exhibits about the park. Along the Lake Superior Shoreline is the Union Bay Campground. It is the park's only modern campground and has about one hundred sites with electricity. The campground also has bathrooms with flush toilets and showers. Nearby is a camp store with some necessities and treats, but I recommend making sure you are stocked up on what you need since it can be a long trip to a town like Ontonagon or Bessemer.

The Lake of the Clouds is the most popular place in the park. It is something you have to see with your own eyes in order to truly take in the beauty of it. The lake lies in a valley, and an overlook provides a stunning view.

Nonesuch

The old mine is located at
46.75581158007238,
-89.61972874433033

Parking on
S Boundary Rd. South of the
Visitors center

Hidden among the trees in the Porcupine Mountains are the ruins of an old mining town. The town of Nonesuch was created when mining near the Little Iron River began in 1867. The town and mine were named for nonesuch, a type of copper ore that exists in sandstone. At its peak, the town had a population of 300 people. Along with the mining buildings, the small town had a school, boarding houses, stables, and even a baseball team. Extracting the fine copper particles out of the sandstone was a labor intensive process, and by 1912, the mine had closed.

Stone walls and cast iron machine parts from the mine can still be found in the area where the town once stood. The best way to get to the ruins is to take South Boundary Road east from the visitors center. Where the road curves south you will find a dirt road that leads to a parking area with some signage for the old mine. A footpath about a half-mile long leads to the historic mine site.

Presque Isle River

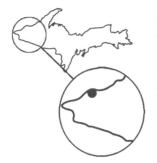

Presque Isle Rd. Western side of Porcupine Mountains Wilderness State Park. 46.70792160887383, -89.97505973078798

The Presque Isle River flows through the western side of the Porcupine Mountains State Park. Manabezho Falls, Manido Falls, and Nawadaha Falls are falls along the river that can be viewed in the park. Near the mouth of the river is a campground, which has about fifty rustic campsites and is split into two loops. The east loop is the generator-friendly side, while the west loop is generator-free for those who are looking for peace and quiet. Not far from the campground is a wooden suspension bridge for hikers to cross over the river and into ninety miles of trails through the vast park's wilderness.

Black River Scenic Byway

Black River National Forest Scenic Byway
46.66472544895035,
-90.04707207353349

The Black River empties into Lake Superior not far from the Wisconsin Border. It has several spectacular waterfalls, including the Great Conglomerate Falls, Potawatomi Falls, Gorge Falls, Sandstone Falls, and Rainbow Falls. Potawatomi Falls and Gorge Falls are near each other, and you can take a short hike along the river between them. Rainbow Falls has

166

about two hundred steps down several staircases to reach the falls. I recommend for a better view of the falls to cross over the river on the suspension bridge in the harbor and then hike back up the river to the falls.

At the mouth of the river is the Black River Harbor managed by the National Forest Service. The harbor has picnic tables and restrooms, but you do need to pay a fee if you do not have an America The Beautiful National Park Pass. A 210-foot suspension bridge was built in 1938 by the Civilian Conservation Corps. It was reconstructed in 1967 and refurbished in 2009. The bridge is part of the North Country Scenic Trail and allows hikers to cross the Black River with a spectacular view as it bounces and sways as you cross it.

An old wooden fishing boat named the *Nancy Jean* sits on display at Black River Harbor. The 32-foot wooden boat powered by a gasoline engine was built in 1913. A fishing village once stood at the mouth of the Black River and in the 1930s, the *Nancy Jean* was used as a commercial fishing boat. In the 1950s, it was used as a charter fishing boat, and then it was pulled up onto land and sat near the location of the long gone fishing village. In 1991, the Ottawa National Forest (they manage the Black River Harbor) purchased the old boat for one dollar. They did some restoration and put it on display as a reminder of days gone by at the harbor.

167

Copper Peak

N13870 Copper Peak Rd.
Ironwood, MI 49938
46.59975105663514,
-90.0881092528028

Along the Black River Scenic Byway you will see a massive structure protruding out over the trees. It is the Copper Peak Ski Jump. It was constructed in 1969 and is the only ski flying facility in the western hemisphere. 1994 was the last year a ski jump event was held at Copper Peak, but money has been raised and the jump is undergoing renovation; there is hope that ski jumpers will be flying off of it soon.

The jump offers visitors rides to the top with a paid ticket. It is extremely popular in autumn when color is at its peak. If the facility is closed when you're there, it is still worth it to take a drive to the parking lot and look at the massive ski jump. One can only think that the people who fly off the jump are insane when you get a look at how massive and high it is.

Old Victoria Townsite

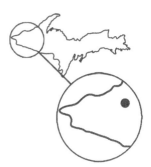

25401 Victoria Dam Rd,
Rockland, MI 49960
46.75861406822873,
-89.23840340199219

Southwest of Rockland is the Old Victoria historic townsite. It was founded in 1899 as a mining town for the Victoria Copper Mining Company. The town was abandoned in 1921, and the buildings fell into disrepair. In 1965, a group of local residents began restoring the townsite, and it is now open to the public as a museum.

The townsite contains several restored buildings, including a schoolhouse, a church, and a general store. There are also several historical exhibits on display. The town offers a unique glimpse into the history of copper mining in the region. It is open daily from June to October.

Skoglund Homestead

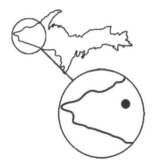

Forest Road 1130 north of Kenton
46.578151677256,
-88.9730197614401

In the heart of the Ottawa National Forest is an old stone cellar dug into the hillside. It was part of the Skoglund Homestead north of Kenton. It sits out in the middle of nowhere in a field of tall grass. It is an interesting and remote trip out to see this historic spot and the old cellar looks like a Hobbit's home. Inside it has concrete walls and floor, and nothing else but dust and dirt. It looks as if it has been a long time since it has been used. The Skoglunds must have been isolated from civilization deep in the woods, but it sure is a beautiful place.

Hiawatha Statue

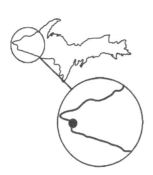 Burma Rd, Ironwood.
MI 49938
46.45140896993529,
-90.16195562913828

The town of Ironwood sits next to the Wisconsin border. About a mile south of downtown is a small park with an enormous statue. It is of Hiawatha, a legendary leader of the Iroquois Confederacy, and a sign below the statue declares it to be the world's tallest Indian. The park is the site of the old

Norrie Iron Mine. The 52-foot-tall fiberglass statue was erected in 1964, and funded by local auto dealer Charlie Gotta. It was built to help draw tourists to travel through downtown Ironwood. I am not sure how much it helped, but it is definitely an attention grabber. The park also has some mining artifacts on display with some information signs about the history of the mine.

Superior Falls

County Rd 505
(Lake Superior Rd.)
power plant access road near
the Montreal River
46.56484820391617,
-90.41526245676032

The Montreal River in the western edge of the UP forms part of the boundary between Michigan and Wisconsin. On the Wisconsin side of the river are the Superior Falls. They can be viewed from the Michigan side at a parking lot of a small hydro electric power plant. If you are ambitious and have strong legs, you can hike down the road next to the power plant to the mouth of the river. It can get steep on the way down. Along the shoreline are plenty of rocks for rock hunters to explore. If you hike back upstream, you can get a spectacular view of the falls from a gorge that the river has cut.

Conclusion

I am sure I missed some places that you may have visited or learned about, but the Upper Peninsula has so many fascinating historical artifacts and natural wonders that nobody could list them all in one book. I am still exploring and discovering new and exciting places in "God's Country", as some people refer to the UP. Making the trip over the Mackinac Bridge and discovering something new is what brings travelers to the UP year after year. There is no way you can possibly see everything in one trip or even one lifetime, but it sure is fun trying.

Other Books by
Mike Sonnenberg

Lost In Michigan
Volumes 1 - 6

Lost In Ohio

Lost In Indiana

I hope you will continue
to follow my journey at

www.lostinmichigan.net

To follow my travels outside of
Michigan you can visit

www.lostinthestates.com

Made in United States
Cleveland, OH
26 April 2025

16447351R00105